The Tough Luck Constitution and the Assault on Health Care Reform

The Tough Luck Constitution and the Assault on Health Care Reform

Andrew Koppelman

OXFORD
UNIVERSITY PRESS

OXFORD
UNIVERSITY PRESS

Oxford University Press is a department of the University of Oxford.
It furthers the University's objective of excellence in research, scholarship,
and education by publishing worldwide.

Oxford   New York
Auckland   Cape Town   Dar es Salaam   Hong Kong   Karachi
Kuala Lumpur   Madrid   Melbourne   Mexico City   Nairobi
New Delhi   Shanghai   Taipei   Toronto

With offices in
Argentina   Austria   Brazil   Chile   Czech Republic   France   Greece
Guatemala   Hungary   Italy   Japan   Poland   Portugal   Singapore
South Korea   Switzerland   Thailand   Turkey   Ukraine   Vietnam

Oxford is a registered trademark of Oxford University Press
in the UK and certain other countries.

Published in the United States of America by
Oxford University Press
198 Madison Avenue, New York, NY 10016

Library of Congress Cataloging-in-Publication Data
Koppelman, Andrew.
The tough luck constitution and the assault on health care reform / Andrew Koppelman.
    pages cm
Includes bibliographical references and index.
ISBN 978–0–19–997002–5 (hardback : alk. paper)   1. National health insurance—
Law and legislation—United States.   2. Health insurance—Law and legislation—United
States.   3. Constitutional law—United States.   4. Health care reform—United States.
5. Medical care—United States.   6. United States. Patient Protection and Affordable
Care Act.   I. Title.
KF3605.K67 2013
344.7302′2—dc23
2012046788

ISBN: 978–0–19–997002–5

9 8 7 6 5 4 3 2 1
Printed in the United States of America
on acid-free paper

For Valerie, Miles, Gina, and Emme

Contents

Acknowledgments

First thanks go to David McBride of Oxford University Press. This book was his idea.

Valuable research assistance was provided by Jonathan Dean, Brandon Mihalisin, Tao Qu, Kaitlyn Quigley, Ariel Simon, and, above all, Marcia Lehr, reference librarian extraordinaire. The Searle Center on Law, Regulation, and Economic Growth hosted a conference on the manuscript in August 2012. Thanks to its director, Max Schanzenbach, coordinator Derek Gunderson, and the participants, Jonathan Adler, Ron Allen, Bob Bennett, Charlotte Crane, Mark Hall, Heidi Kitrosser, Eugene Kontorovich, David Kopel, John Ohlendorf, Steve Presser, Neil Siegel, Nadav Shoked, and Ilya Somin. Special thanks to Profs. Kopel and Somin for repeatedly pressing me with smart objections by email after the conference. A writer's best friends are those who frankly bring him the bad news.

I am also grateful for comments from Bruce Ackerman, Jack Balkin, Randy Barnett, David Bernstein, Josh Blackman, Steve Calabresi, Tony D'Amato, Senator Tom Daschle, Erin Delaney, Richard Epstein, Brian Glassman, Linda Greenhouse, Mark Hall, Tim Jost, Orin Kerr, Rogan Kersh, Margaret Koppelman,

Kurt Lash, Simon Lazarus, Adam Liptak, David McBride, John McGinnis, Valerie Quinn, Martin Redish, Stephen Siegel, Paul Starr, Ron Suskind, Mark Tushnet, and Peter Urbanowicz, and to helpful conversations with Jonathan Cohn, Peter DiCola, Zev Eigen, Joey Fishkin, Josh Kleinfeld, Gary Lawson, Hashim Moopaan, Eugene Volokh, and Dan Wikler.

My interest in this topic began when I was invited to debate the constitutional issue with Peter Urbanowicz at the American Health Lawyers Association annual meeting in December 2010.

In an exchange in the *Yale Law Journal Online*, Gary Lawson and David Kopel pointed out errors in some of my arguments, which I have corrected (though doubtless not to their satisfaction).

Steve Lubet has been my invaluable mentor and friend throughout this project. In one of our many conversations, he coined the term "tough luck libertarianism," devised the "can't think of another" critique, and likely is responsible for other ideas herein for which I have forgotten to credit him. Thanks also to Northwestern Law School's dean, Dan Rodriguez, director of research Jide Nzelibe, and my assistant, Jane Brock, for their unflagging and generous support.

Parts of this book previously appeared in the Balkinization blog, the *Yale Law Journal Online*, *Constitutional Commentary*, Salon.com, and the *New Republic Online*.

The Tough Luck Constitution and the Assault on Health Care Reform

Introduction

In a revealing moment during the March 2012 Supreme Court argument over the constitutionality of President Barack Obama's health care reform law, Solicitor General Donald Verrilli argued that the state legitimately could compel Americans to purchase health insurance because the country is obligated to pay for the uninsured when they get sick.

Justice Antonin Scalia responded: "Well, don't obligate yourself to that."[1]

One wonders what Verrilli thought of this. Scalia was saying, in effect, that there is no real *obligation* to care for sick people who cannot afford to pay for their own medical care; that any assumed "obligation" is really a discretionary choice. You can choose to obligate yourself or not.

Verrilli replied that the Constitution did not "forbid Congress from taking into account this deeply embedded social norm." Scalia didn't argue with that, but he still was not satisfied. A bit later, he suggested that under the Constitution, "the people were left to decide whether they want to buy insurance or not." This would mean that any federally required insurance scheme was unconstitutional. It would invalidate Medicare and Social Security. Scalia clearly did not mean that. But then, why was he saying these things?

Comments like these stunned many legal analysts and led them to quickly revise their view that the law would easily be upheld. Most prominent was CNN reporter Jeffrey Toobin: "This law looks like it's going to be struck down. I'm telling you, all of the predictions, including mine, that the justices would not have a problem with this law were wrong. I think this law is in grave, grave trouble."[2]

Then the law was upheld, by a bare 5–4 majority. Chief Justice John Roberts cast the deciding vote, but he also announced a bunch of surprising new restrictions on congressional power. He implied that universal health care would be unconstitutional: Congress couldn't compel it under its commerce power, and incentives under the taxing power would only be permissible if they were somewhat ineffective. Most important, he declared that states have a constitutional right to decline the act's expansion of federal Medicaid assistance for the poor. The four dissenters agreed with that, but they wanted to strike down the entire statute, including parts that they admitted presented no constitutional problem.

The constitutional challenge to the Patient Protection and Affordable Care Act of 2010 (the ACA for short) was devised by conservative lawyers who had, for a long time, been eager to have the Court impose limits on congressional power. They invented the objections as the bill was nearing passage. Republican leaders, facing a humiliating political defeat, seized on those arguments as their last hope. They weren't much concerned about the details: two weeks after publication of the first, underdeveloped draft of the constitutional argument, every Republican Senator voted to endorse it. That argument's central claim was that the state can't make you do things; that it may regulate only those who engage in some self-initiated action. It creatively read into the Constitution the notion that the law's trivial burden on individuals was intolerable, even when the alternative was a regime in which millions were needlessly denied decent medical care. The action/inaction distinction came advertised as a great bulwark of liberty. Actually, it was a crude bit of political opportunism. No one can live in the world without engaging in self-initiated actions all the time. If that's all it takes to trigger regulation, then government can push its citizens around in nearly any way it likes while scrupulously respecting the action/inaction distinction.

The ACA's so-called individual mandate, which required nearly everyone to purchase health insurance, is in practice a penalty or a tax—as we shall see, it matters a lot what you call it—that must be paid by those who fail to carry a minimum level of health insurance coverage.[3] It was the focus of challenges to the law. A central purpose of the ACA was to extend insurance to people with preexisting medical conditions, whom insurers had become very efficient at keeping off their rolls. This group includes not only sick people but anyone likely to file an expensive medical claim, such as women of childbearing age.

How many Americans have preexisting medical conditions? Estimates vary wildly, ranging from 20% to 66% of the adult population. (The uninsured report fewer such conditions, because their problems are likely to be undetected.) In the first quarter of 2010, 19% of applicants in the individual market were denied enrollment, and a quarter of insurers had denial rates of 40% or more.[4]

A rule against discriminating against those people, standing alone, would mean that healthy people could wait until they get sick to buy insurance. Because insurance pools rely on cross-subsidization of sick people by healthy participants, that would bankrupt the entire individual insurance market. Massachusetts, acting a few years before the federal law, combined its guarantee of coverage with a mandate, but seven other states tried to protect people with preexisting conditions without mandating coverage for everyone. The results in those states ranged from huge premium increases to the complete collapse of the market. In New York, for example, the individual market dropped from 752,000 covered persons in 1994 to 34,000 in 2009.[5]

Scalia suggested that there was no real difficulty: "You could solve that problem by simply not requiring the insurance company to sell it to somebody who has a condition that is going to require medical treatment, or at least not—not require them to sell it to him at a rate that he sells it to healthy people." In other words, you can solve the problem by deciding that it isn't a problem. Once more, assuring that everyone has insurance may be something that government is simply not permitted to do.

Why would that be impermissible? Justice Anthony Kennedy explained:

[T]he reason this is concerning is because it requires the individual to do an affirmative act. In the law of torts, our tradition, our law has been that you don't have the duty to rescue someone if that person is in danger. The blind man is walking in front of a car and you do not have a duty to stop him, absent some relation between you. And there is some severe moral criticisms [sic] of that rule, but that's generally the rule.

And here the government is saying that the Federal Government has a duty to tell the individual citizen that it must act, and that is different from what we have in previous cases, and that changes the relationship of the Federal Government to the individual in a very fundamental way.

Kennedy seems to think that the old common-law rule of no duty to rescue—one which, he acknowledges, is morally dubious—could be a matter of fundamental right, such that there is some constitutional impediment to changing it. And this impediment comes into play not only when someone is required to engage in some physical act but when someone is required to pay money for someone else's benefit.

Justice Samuel Alito, offering a different objection to the law, thought it "artificial to say that somebody who is doing absolutely nothing about health care is financing health care services" and demanded that the United States concede that "what this mandate is really doing is not requiring the people who are subject to it to pay for the services that they are going to consume? It is requiring them to subsidize services that will be received by somebody else."[6] Justice Ruth Bader Ginsburg responded: "If you're going to have insurance, that's how insurance works." But Ginsburg's response was not necessarily devastating.

It depends on what kind of thing health care is: Is it a basic right, something that should be available to everyone regardless of their health and wealth, or is it an ordinary commodity? If it is the latter, then Scalia, Kennedy, and Alito are right: it is fair to make everyone pay for their own coverage, and insurers should make their customers pay premiums in line with the risks they represent.[7] If you are too poor to buy medical treatment or health insurance, tough luck: you can't get something in a market unless you pay for it. If you have been sick in the past, that's tough luck, too: your insurance will be ruinously expensive, and the policy won't cover the illnesses you are most likely to get.

Government efforts to help you would be an outrageous violation of liberty. Call this Tough Luck Libertarianism.

Markets are normally good for consumers. Providers compete to provide high-quality products at low prices. But insurance markets are different.

An insurer profits by taking in a lot of premiums and paying out as little as possible in claims. In health insurance, that means there is an incentive to restrict one's pool of customers to young, healthy people and to cancel the policy of anyone who gets really sick. The least expensive 50% of health consumers account for only 3% of the costs. The most costly 10% account for 70% of the costs.[8] So competitive pressures move the system toward denying care to those who most need it. Insurers who become skillful at protecting themselves from large payouts—by excluding coverage for preexisting conditions, by denying claims or delaying payment, and by raising rates or canceling policies for individuals who become sick—will financially outperform their competitors. They are behaving rationally, in ways that a well-functioning market will reward.[9] As I will explain in chapter 1, in the United States, where health care is provided by private insurers, these incentives have created a system in which more and more people are squeezed out.

The other view is that everyone has a right to health care.[10] Some members of the community are too poor to purchase that care, too sick to be insurable, or both. They will only get care if the responsibility for paying for that care is shared by the society as a whole. That means some system of social insurance, of a kind that exists in every rich democracy in the world except the United States.

If you think there's a right to health care, the American health care system before Obama was fundamentally broken. About 15% of Americans had no health insurance in 2008, and the number was growing. About three-quarters of these people work, more than half of them full-time. Coverage has eroded slightly for employees in the top two-fifths of earners, but more than 90% of them remain covered. The middle fifth has gone from 5% to 12.4% uninsured since 1980. The next-to-bottom fifth has gone from less than 10% to 21.9% uninsured, and the bottom fifth has more than doubled, from 18% to 37.4%.[11]

The uninsured suffered avoidable illness, received less preventive care, were diagnosed when their illnesses were more advanced, and once diagnosed received less therapeutic care. The Institute of Medicine estimated that having health insurance would reduce their mortality rates by 10 to 25%.[12] For example, women without insurance are nearly 50% more likely to die of breast cancer, because their tumors are not diagnosed at an early stage.[13] Estimates of deaths from lack of health insurance vary wildly, but range as high as 45,000.[14] Those who don't die are in worse health, and sometimes are financially ruined by medical expenses.

If there is to be a right to health care, the money has to come from somewhere. Unlike many other rights, this one can't be enforced just by making government leave people alone. A person bleeding to death on the sidewalk is being left alone by the government.

One option is to tax citizens directly, as is done with Social Security and Medicare. Another is to mandate that businesses provide the services to those who cannot afford to pay and pass on the cost to their customers who can; that was once done voluntarily by insurers and hospitals, before competitive pressures made them stop, and it happens now when emergency rooms are required to treat indigent patients (though those hospitals are also quite willing to dun uninsured patients for thousands of dollars). Tax incentives can be provided for the purchase of insurance.

Employers can be required to provide insurance (though this discourages new hiring, is hard on small businesses, and is no help to the unemployed). The ACA's mandate is just another technique for financing broad coverage, adopted, despite its unpopularity, because all the others had proved politically impossible or practically inadequate.

The choice between these two views, commodity and shared responsibility, has for a long time been a political one, and American health policy has been about intermediate possibilities.[15] The ACA moves in the direction of shared responsibility, but there is still plenty of scope for the commodity model: rich people will continue to get better care than poor ones, and policies will be cheaper for the healthy than for the sick.

What was radical about the suggestions of Scalia, Kennedy, and Alito was their implication that the choice between these two models is not appropriately a matter for politics at all, that fundamental fairness is violated by the idea of a right to health care. Does the Constitution require Tough Luck Libertarianism? That would have implications that go far beyond the mandate. If it is unjust to require anyone to subsidize anyone else, then even the graduated income tax (which, inconveniently, the Sixteenth Amendment authorizes) would have to go. If someone is indigent and in need of medical care, that person might perhaps be aided by private charity, but it would be unjust for the state to commandeer taxpayer dollars to aid him or her, or to require private parties to do so. Scalia's "don't obligate yourself to that" is phrased in the imperative. It itself states a moral obligation.

What conception of justice could require that surprising result? Here we need to briefly review the most famous debate in modern political philosophy. The shared-responsibility view has been most thoroughly worked out by the Harvard philosopher John Rawls. The ordinary-commodity view was defended by his colleague Robert Nozick. Comparing them can help us understand what is at stake in the debate over the mandate.

Rawls is the most sophisticated modern proponent of social contract theory—a tradition going back to Hobbes, Locke, and Rousseau. He proposed that society should be seen as a scheme of cooperation among equals. In order for the social contract to be fair, its terms should be devised without any of the parties knowing their position in society, most relevantly whether they would be rich or poor. With their information thus restricted, Rawls argued that the parties would agree only to those inequalities that benefited the least well-off. There could be a capitalist economy, but its fruits would have to be shared with the poor, by redistributive taxation and other such measures.[16] He eventually concluded that this would mean a right to health care.[17] No one would agree to a social contract in which property rights were distributed in a way that might leave her without needed medical resources. Rawls became the preeminent philosophical defender of the welfare state.

Nozick's response likewise made him the most prominent modern theorist of Tough Luck Libertarianism. He objected that Rawls was insufficiently respectful of liberty and property. Rawls would violate people's property rights and continually meddle with free agreements among citizens in order to support a preconceived pattern of distribution. A state should protect citizens from force and fraud, enforce contracts (perhaps even contracts to sell oneself into slavery), and do nothing more. Under no circumstances should it interfere with the existing distribution of property except to rectify past violations of property rights.[18]

The nasty implications of Nozick's views are clear. The state is morally required to let people die of treatable illnesses, or be bankrupted by them; it may not expend any tax dollars to help them. But Nozick has also made a philosophical error. His criticism rests on a fundamental misunderstanding of Rawls, who is asking what property rights there ought to be in the first place. Nozick presupposes that we already know which existing property holdings are morally justified. He also thinks that taking even a penny from a millionaire in some way violates him. The classic one-sentence response to Nozick is George Kateb's: "I find it impossible to conceive of us as having nerve endings in every dollar of our estate."[19] Rawls makes no such assumption. His claim is that institutions such as property should be designed with their likely distributional consequences in mind. "Redistribution" mislabels what Rawls is proposing. His claim is that institutions that guarantee a fair share for the least well-off, such as taxation to support free public schools, are properly part of—not an exception to—the system of property rights.

Many Americans depend for their health care not merely on traditional forms of property but on institutional guarantees, often supported by taxation. They regard such guarantees as *theirs*, and thus inarticulately partake of the more sophisticated, Rawlsian understanding. This is evident even when they oppose reform: consider the infamous statement to a congressman to "keep your government hands off my Medicare."[20] The fundamental error of Tough Luck Libertarianism is that it takes existing property rights (and only those of the old-fashioned sort) for granted and fetishizes them, instead of recognizing property as an institution constructed by human beings for human ends, the details of which can and should be specified with those ends in mind.[21]

Nonetheless, Tough Luck Libertarianism has a powerful hold on the American imagination. Nozick rejected the claim that government should pay for medical care, because it "ignores the question of where the things or actions to be allocated and distributed come from." Any resources that society might devote to medical care already belong to "people who therefore may decide for themselves to whom they will give the thing and on what grounds."[22] His assumptions underlie the statements by the three justices we just quoted—all of whom, as it turned out, wanted to strike down the entire ACA. The sick and poor have no legitimate claim on the property of the rich and healthy (Scalia). There is no duty to aid others, and government efforts to compel such aid, even by extracting money, violate citizens' rights (Kennedy). No one should have to subsidize anyone else (Alito).

Almost no one is a serious Tough Luck Libertarian. Those who make Nozick-like claims typically do so in a baldly selective way, when someone proposes to diminish their own share of the pie to benefit someone else. Then redistribution, from which the speaker usually benefits in multiple ways, becomes an intolerable intrusion on liberty. So there is a dilemma for those who invoke Nozickian arguments. You can invoke them consistently, in which case you end American civilization as we know it. Or you can invoke them only opportunistically, in which case you won't deserve to be taken seriously. The judges and attorneys who sought to invalidate the ACA faced this dilemma. They typically responded by grabbing the second horn—a constitutional limit tailored to do in the ACA, which would probably never be relevant again.

Not all libertarianism is Tough Luck Libertarianism. You can believe in vastly reduced regulation of markets while thinking that there's nothing inherently just about the way they distribute property. Friedrich Hayek, the leading proponent of this view, endorsed Rawls without inconsistency.[23] The concerns raised by Scalia, Kennedy, and Alito are Nozickian, not Hayekian.

Nozick's neo-Kantian emphasis on rule following rather than consequences entailed that the tough results just didn't matter: any effort to ameliorate them would violate citizens' rights.[24] This indifference to consequences was dramatically displayed by libertarian blogger Sasha Volokh, who argued that it would be immoral to tax people to prevent an asteroid from destroying the earth.[25] (The only legitimate function of government is to prevent violations of rights, and accidents, such as the destruction of the earth, are like diseases; they do not violate anyone's rights.)

Most people care about results and must somehow reconcile themselves to them. One response is to own up to the toughness. At a September 2011 Republican presidential debate, when moderator Wolf Blitzer asked libertarian Ron Paul whether, if an uninsured patient goes into a coma, "are you saying that society should just let him die?" Before Paul could answer, some members of the audience shouted "Yes!"[26] But this is rare. A more common view—call it Tragic Antistatism—holds that there's some tough luck that we just have to live with. People sometimes lose out in a market, but if the state intervenes, the effects on incentives will be disastrous, citizens' self-reliant character will be sapped, and everyone will be worse off. It's a mistake to think that there can be a society in which everyone has adequate medical care, and a bigger mistake to try to bring that about.

The soundness of Tragic Antistatism is beyond the scope of this book, since it has nothing to do with constitutional law. I will note, however, that every other rich country has in fact succeeded in bringing about universal health care, without destructive unintended results. France is not North Korea. America has a comparative advantage in generating new medical technologies, so one could reasonably worry about the effect of a larger government role on that. But the ACA's mandate and Medicaid expansion merely push additional people into an otherwise unchanged system, and no one has explained how that could have any negative effect on the progress of medical science.

Tragic Antistatism is a tough sell, because Americans like happy endings. If you want to hang on to your minimal-state convictions, there is another strategy: pretending that you aren't being so tough after all. You can claim that the bad results aren't happening, or will be cured by an unregulated market. The trouble with this solution is that it is contradicted by the evidence, some of which I have already cited. Call this the Tinkerbell strategy, after a famous fictional episode of medical treatment. At one point in the musical adaptation of *Peter Pan*, Tinkerbell the fairy has been poisoned, prompting the following speech by Peter to the audience:

> Tink! Dear Tink! You're dying. Your light is growing faint. If it goes out, that means you're dead. Your voice is so low I can scarcely hear what you're saying. You think that—what, Tink?—you could get well again if children believed in fairies. (facing audience) Do you believe? Oh, please, please believe! If you believe, wherever you are, clap your hands, and she'll hear you. Clap! Clap! Don't let Tink die! Clap! She's getting better! Clap! Clap! She's getting stronger! Oh, she's all well now! Oh, thank you! Thank you![27]

It is almost impossible to discuss health care in the United States without constantly encountering Tinkerbell. One prominent example came from then president George W. Bush in 2007: "[P]eople have access to health care in America. After all, you just go to an emergency room."[28] This is, of course, a massively inefficient way of addressing the problem, which impairs care for real emergencies, sometimes with fatal results.[29] And of course emergency rooms don't provide regular exams or chemotherapy, or refill the prescription you need to stay alive. Another Tinkerbell tactic is to claim that private charity will take care of the problem. Paul's actual answer to the question was to say that when he was a doctor, "[w]e never turned anybody away from the hospitals. . . .

And we've given up on this whole concept that we might take care of ourselves and assume responsibility for ourselves. Our neighbors, our friends, our churches would do it." But if private charity were going to solve the problem, this would already have happened. There is an old joke in which two economists are walking down the street, one says, "Isn't that a twenty-dollar bill on the sidewalk?," and the other replies, "Obviously not, or else someone would already have picked it up." The argument here implies a similar response if you see someone dying on the sidewalk: they're not really there, or else someone would already have taken care of them. Medical care is in reality too expensive for private charity to handle. (Private charity did it in 1900, but per capita medical expenditure was then $5, which is $100 in present dollars. In 2010 it was $8,402.)[30] Market competition puts pressure even on nonprofit and religious hospitals to minimize their volume of charity cases.[31] In different ways, Bush and Paul are both dispensing fistfuls of fairy dust.

A more serious claim, which however has often degenerated into a sophisticated form of Tinkerbell, is the idea of consumer-driven health care. In its more extreme formulations, it claims that all the present ills of the health care system can be cured by giving consumers better information and forcing them to pay more costs out of pocket. On this view, the ACA moves in exactly the wrong direction by expanding the government's role in the health care system. Proponents of consumer-driven health care are a kind of libertarian—they envision a radically diminished regulatory role for government—but they are not Tough Luck Libertarians. Almost all of them support state subsidies for medical care for the poorest citizens. They think that state-directed medical care is likely to be worse medical care, and that their preferred policies would deliver better care than the ACA ever could.

Informed consumer behavior is of course key to the normal functioning of markets. There are elements of consumer-driven health care in the ACA, the most important being the state insurance exchanges where private companies compete. But the health care market is less transparent than most. Even more than with used cars, consumers can't discern the quality of what they are buying. That's a problem when they consume medical services, and even more of a problem when they buy insurance, where what they are purchasing is the future behavior of the insurer. Shifting costs to consumers sometimes worsens health and raises costs because high copayments can deter routine visits to the doctor, thereby preventing early detection of illness. The consumer-driven model, when it is offered as a general prescription for health care reform, relies upon an oversimplified model of how people make decisions. Its distributive implications are also worth noting, although not often advertised: it would shift health care costs from the healthy to the chronically ill.[32]

Whatever the merits of consumer-driven health reform, it is psychologically indispensable to the constitutional objections to the ACA because it purports to show that cutting back on insurance will actually be good for you. Psychologically, but not logically: the consumer-driven theory has nothing to do with constitutional law. The objections that were available to constitutional critics of the ACA—objections we shall consider in detail in chapters 3 and 4—assert constitutional limits that would exist even if there were no other way to deliver medical care to everyone. The dissenters in the ACA declared that the Constitution "contains no whatever-it-takes-to-solve-a-national-problem power." They were committed, by the logic of their position, to a Constitution under which some problems could not be solved by anyone—not the states, not the federal government. They would have struck down the ACA even if it were the only way to achieve near-universal health care.

This is why so many people (including, perhaps, some Supreme Court justices) who were not Tough Luck Libertarians at all, who would find that philosophy repellent, nonetheless found themselves saying Tough Luck Libertarian things and, in the opinion they finally wrote, making claims based on a Tough Luck *Constitution*—a constitution in which there is no realistic path to universal health care. That Constitution won't be attractive unless Tough Luck Libertarianism is right that it is acceptable to deny people the medical care they need. The challengers to the ACA talked a lot about slippery slopes—at the bottom of this one was a law requiring you to buy broccoli—but there's a slope in the other direction as well. Once you decide that it's acceptable to hold your nose and make this kind of argument, it will be easier next time.

We have not yet discussed the specific legal arguments against the ACA, which concern the scope of the congressional power to regulate commerce, the taxing power, and individual liberty to make economic and medical decisions. We shall do so in chapters 3 and 4. Their persuasiveness depends on confusion about both the rationale for the mandate and the limitations that the Constitution actually imposes on congressional power. This book therefore examines both before turning to the legal arguments.

Chapter 1 examines the history of health care reform in America and shows how the logic of reform led Congress to choose the mandate over other, functionally equivalent but politically impossible ways of delivering near-universal health care. Chapter 2 describes the appropriate constitutional limitations on congressional power, limitations that are no impediment to the mandate. Chapter 3 shows when and how the constitutional objections were devised. Chapter 4 examines the Court's decision. Chapter 5 considers the decision's aftermath.

ONE

The Road to the Mandate

The most politically toxic aspect of the mandate, it became clear at oral argument, is that it requires some people to subsidize others. This is, however, an inevitable aspect of any system, with or without purchase mandates, that guarantees decent health care for everyone. The basic idea was succinctly stated by President Harry Truman: "If instead of the costs of sickness being paid only by those who get sick, all the people—sick and well— were required to pay premiums into an insurance fund, the pool of funds thus created would enable all who do fall sick to be adequately served without overburdening anyone."[1]

The Obama mandate is only one of many mechanisms by which this cross-subsidization can occur. Obama understood perfectly well that it was an unpopular way of doing it. He had made use of its unpopularity himself against Hillary Clinton in the Democratic primaries. By the time he was actually devising a law as president, however, it became clear that no other method of cross-subsidization was politically possible. All these methods were functional equivalents. How could it make a constitutional difference which of them was used?

ORIGINS OF HEALTH INSURANCE

Government efforts to guarantee health care date back to 1790, when Congress required ship owners to buy medical insurance for their seamen. (President George Washington signed it into law.) In 1798, it enacted the first individual mandate, requiring the seamen to buy hospital insurance for themselves.[2] Both of these laws followed a long-standing English custom of providing health care for sailors.

The first government-provided health care program involving large domestic populations was instituted in Germany in 1883 by Chancellor Otto von Bismarck, who hoped thereby to take an issue away from the political Left. Participation was compulsory for industrial workers; employers and workers both contributed to the fund.[3] The American Socialist Party first endorsed compulsory health insurance in 1904, but it was a minor party with little impact. More important was the Progressive Party's endorsement of the idea in 1912, when Theodore Roosevelt, formerly the Republican president, was its candidate (although he never discussed the issue).

The late nineteenth century also saw the beginning of rising medical costs. Licensing of doctors began, raising quality but also price. Hospitals had previously been conducted on a charitable basis, mainly for the poor, but antiseptic surgery and other advances made them attractive to all social classes. Hospital stays became increasingly expensive, sometimes beyond the means of middle-class families.

In the late 1920s and 1930s, hospitals and hospital associations created the first health insurance plans. These eventually evolved into Blue Cross, a network of nonprofit plans.[4] The earliest forms of Blue Cross themselves acted as a form of social insurance. In the early twentieth century, virtually all health insurance policies were Blue Cross plans. By 1938, they had enrolled 2.8 million people.[5] Such policies were community rated: everyone paid the same price, old or young, healthy or sick. "Community rating" means that some people pay more than their average cost, while others pay less. The consequence was cross-subsidization. But beginning in the late 1940s, commercial insurers began to enter the market, setting their premiums by "experience rating," based on each person's age and past health history. This meant lower rates for younger and healthier people, who thus were easily drawn away from Blue Cross. The private insurers became very profitable, and Blue Cross enrollment fell, with rising premiums because its average patient was older and sicker. By 1952, commercial enrollment exceeded that of Blue Cross, and by 1958, Blue Cross had a $40 million deficit. Blue Cross had always made community rating one of its core principles, but by the late 1950s, most Blues had to switch to experience rating. Since then, health insurance has been experience rated almost everywhere except in states that prohibit it.[6]

In the original Blue Cross approach, everyone contributed equally to a pool that was administered not by the government but by a nonprofit corporation. This is unsustainable in a free market. A business that relies on some of its customers to subsidize others is always at risk of having competitors draw away the subsidizers. Market forces also introduce administrative costs: medical underwriting, the practice of scrutinizing each applicant to determine eligibility and premiums, is expensive, and that expense gets passed on as increased premiums. When Congress passed the ACA, it found that administrative expenses were 26 to 30% of premiums in individual and small group markets.

Franklin Roosevelt considered health insurance along with the other New Deal reforms, but he feared that it would sink Social Security and unemployment insurance. He never did press for it, or provide any specifics about what kind of coverage he had in mind. His main contribution to American health care was an unexpected by-product of wage and price controls during World War II. The War Labor Board ruled that employer-provided health insurance did not count as wages. This gave employers in tight labor markets a way of competing for workers. It also meant that such insurance wasn't taxed as income.[7] It's not clear how much the war policy had to do with the wartime growth in coverage, most of which happened before the Labor Board policy took effect.[8] There are economic advantages to employer-based coverage, having to do with economies of scale and the creation of natural risk pools. The tax policy deepened and accelerated them. In 1940, 12 million Americans had health insurance. By 1950, the number was 76.6 million, more than half the U.S. population, and was growing rapidly. By 1960, 122 million Americans had private health insurance.[9] So in a backhanded and unintended way, Roosevelt helped to deliver health insurance to a majority of Americans. What's more, for large employers, insurance was community rated across all employees, creating cross-subsidization.

Because employer-provided insurance is community rated, but individual insurance remains experience rated, the labor market was distorted. A worker with a history of illness, or whose family members had such a history, had an incentive to find a large employer to work for and to stay on that employer's payroll. Thus began "job lock," the pressure to keep one's job even if one could otherwise be better employed elsewhere—a phenomenon that, when the ACA was enacted, affected approximately a quarter of American workers.[10] Job lock was a particular disincentive to starting a small business, for which only experience-rated insurance is available. A corresponding, less quantifiable burden is "marriage lock": people are reluctant to leave marriages, even some pretty bad ones, when it may mean losing their health care.

Truman was the first president to support single-payer, comprehensive, compulsory insurance. The American Medical Association (AMA), prepared to do battle with any government health program—it has since changed radically, and supported the ACA—declared that "Truman's health insurance plan would make doctors slaves" and called his staff "followers of the Moscow party line."[11] It faked a quotation from Lenin, "Socialized medicine is the keystone to the arch of the socialist state," which was repeated frequently in the fight over Obama's bill sixty years later.[12]

"Public choice" theory claims that any significant governmental intervention is likely to be captured by special interests, which will then deploy governmental power to benefit themselves. This argument for a minimal government role in the economy is popular among Tough Luck Libertarians. But it is manifestly contradicted by the facts, notably that the air you're breathing and the water you're drinking are both a lot cleaner than they were when the Environmental Protection Agency was created in 1970.[13]

Health care shows how special interests can sometimes be served by Tough Luck Libertarianism. For many years, the AMA opposed any substantial government role in medical care, evidently with the goal of maximizing physician incomes. In the Great Depression, many people were unable to afford medical services. In 1934, the incoming AMA president recommended closing half the country's medical schools, thereby constricting the supply of medical care and raising its price. That same year, the AMA's Council of Medical Education warned about admitting too many students, and medical school admissions declined for the next six years, at a time when there was a desperate need for more medical care.[14] In 1964, when President Lyndon Johnson's Medicare bill seemed likely to narrowly pass in the House Ways and Means Committee, the AMA misrepresented scientific facts in order to buy the vote of a key member. It deemed "inconclusive" the new Surgeon General's report on the dangers of smoking, which found that heavy smokers were twenty times as likely to get lung cancer as nonsmokers. It announced that it had accepted $10 million from six tobacco companies in order to study the issue. An AMA publication acknowledged that some researchers found that smoking was dangerous, but it declared that "equally competent physicians and research personnel are less sure of the effect of cigarette smoking on health.... They advise, 'Smoke if you feel you should, but be moderate.'" The day before the committee vote, a Kentucky congressman from a tobacco-growing district withdrew his support and so killed the bill. The AMA was willing to misinform the public about deadly dangers in order to prevent national health insurance.[15] It was so resistant to political encroachment that it opposed compulsory vaccination against smallpox and diphtheria.[16] Sometimes regulatory capture produces small government.

Truman's bill died, but one of its parts, the 1946 Hill-Burton bill for hospital construction, passed easily, because it gave state legislators money to build new hospitals in their districts.[17] It included a requirement, ignored for decades thereafter, that hospitals constructed with its funds devote "a reasonable amount of services" to those unable to pay.[18] (Implementing regulations, which actually forced hospitals to take some indigent patients, were promulgated in 1979.)[19] By the end of his presidency, Truman was persuaded to pursue the more incremental goal of insurance for Americans over age sixty-four. Thus began the movement toward Medicare.

The period after World War II also saw the beginning of exploding health care costs. Between 1948 and 1958, per capita health spending increased by 82%; out-of-pocket spending rose 48%, but payments by insurance companies rose by 442%.[20] This generated pressure for federal intervention, but for a long time nothing was done. President Dwight Eisenhower said he would veto any Medicare legislation as "a definite step toward socialized medicine."[21] Ronald Reagan warned in 1961 that if Medicare was enacted, "one of these days you and I are going to spend our sunset years telling our children, and our children's children, what it once was like in America when men were free."[22] There was also resistance from southern legislators, who feared that federal involvement would force them to racially integrate hospitals and other health care facilities.[23]

Pressure grew for health insurance for the elderly. In 1958, medical expenses for Americans over age sixty-five were more than twice those of younger Americans. In 1962, only 38% of nonworking elderly, and 37% of those who described themselves as in poor health, had any health insurance.[24] In 1961, insurance was paying about 7% of the total medical bills of the elderly.[25]

AFTER MEDICARE AND MEDICAID

The big breakthrough, and the biggest expansion of government-funded health care in American history—far bigger than the ACA—was the establishment of Medicare and Medicaid in 1965. Medicare provided single-payer coverage for everyone over sixty-five. It, together with increasingly generous Social Security benefits, fundamentally transformed what it meant to be old in America. Before then, declining health often meant crushing medical bills. In 1962, slightly more than half of the elderly had any health insurance.[26] By 1970, the figure was close to 100%. The elderly poverty rate declined from 28.5% in 1965 to 15.3% in 1975 and 9% in 2010.[27] Medicare also however divided access to health insurance by age, which no other country does.[28]

Medicaid was less effective. The 1965 legislation created two tiers of separate and unequal benefits, with Medicaid payment rates so low that many doctors would not take Medicaid patients.[29] It provided coverage for the very poor and disabled, though because the program was administered by the states, there were enormous variations in eligibility. In Alabama in 2009, it covered families with children who had incomes below 11.5% of the federal poverty line, which was $2,425.50 a year for a family of four.[30]

The 1965 legislation nonetheless was an enormous transformation. Most Americans now had protection against the financial risks of illness. The money for these programs came from taxation, with those who earned more paying more.

After Johnson, liberals led by Senator Edward Kennedy sought to expand Medicare to make single-payer coverage available to everyone. Richard Nixon embraced the goal of universal health insurance. To counter Kennedy, he proposed a mandate for all employers to offer health insurance to their full-time employees, with subsidized coverage for every citizen not covered by employers. Nixon did not include an individual mandate. He accomplished cost-spreading with the subsidies, funded out of general revenues. His plans ended when the Watergate scandal forced him to resign.[31] Gerald Ford did not resubmit Nixon's plan to Congress, saying it would worsen inflation.[32] Jimmy Carter supported a plan much like Nixon's. Neither Ronald Reagan nor George H. W. Bush showed much interest in universal coverage. Bush's chief of staff, John Sununu, told one economist, "If the American people want health care, they'll vote for Democrats."[33] The most significant expansion of health care in this period was the 1986 Emergency Medical Treatment and Active Labor Act, which requires hospital emergency rooms to take all patients in need of urgent care regardless of ability to pay. This achieved some cross-subsidization: about 20% of emergency room patients are uninsured,[34] forcing hospitals to raise their rates for everyone else. However, the law had the unintended effect of creating pressure to close emergency rooms altogether.

By the late 1980s, the prospect of comprehensive health care reform had disappeared. When Representative Claude Pepper, who had been advocating health care since the New Deal, died in 1989, Democrats told each other that when he arrived in heaven, he asked whether America would ever have national health insurance, and God said, "Yes, but not in my lifetime."[35]

Yet the status quo was unsustainable. Health care costs continued to grow much faster than the economy—from $256 billion in 1980 to $724 billion in 1990;[36] from 9.3% of GDP in 1980 to 13.6% in 1992.[37] During the same period, health insurance premiums increased, on average, by 300%.[38] Per capita health care spending grew from $1,100 in 1980 to $2,854 in 1990.[39] As costs rose, health care was increasingly out of reach, or financially devastating, for those without insurance.

By the time Bill Clinton tried to enact comprehensive reform, the American health care system had become a patchwork. Anyone who worries about American health care becoming like that of other countries should notice that each of the world's different financing approaches is already represented somewhere in the current system. For most working people under sixty-five, health care is like that in Germany or France or Japan, where worker and employer share the cost of privately provided health insurance. For Native Americans, the military, and veterans, government employs doctors and maintains clinics and hospitals to provide free care, as in Britain or Cuba. For those over sixty-five, government pays for privately provided medical care, as in Canada. And for the uninsured, medical care is available for those who pay out of pocket, as in Cambodia or other impoverished countries.[40]

Clinton tried to enact universal coverage and failed spectacularly. He faced a different problem than Truman or Johnson, because employment-based insurance and Medicare had changed political conditions. When the majority, and the most politically vocal parts of the majority, have full protection, then it is hard to expand further.[41] The development of American health care has involved the selective extension of health insurance to slivers of the population that were either unusually politically powerful, unusually sympathetic, or both. The reforms generated what Paul Starr calls a "policy trap": so many people were given a stake in the new status quo that further change, in the direction of universal health care, became extremely difficult.[42] (Whether it counted as a policy trap depends, of course, on one's goal. If you think that the present system is just fine, then political paralysis is fine as well. If you're a Tough Luck Libertarian, then you face a different kind of policy trap, because it's so hard to abolish Medicare, Medicaid, and other redistributive measures.)

Clinton fell squarely into the trap. Most Americans are satisfied with the health insurance they have. Yet his central idea was to have all insurance funneled through new health insurance purchasing cooperatives, which would negotiate with insurance companies and then present a menu of options to their customers. A national health board would administer a global budget. Employers could no longer purchase coverage directly; they would have to purchase through the cooperatives instead. Small employers that did not provide insurance for their employees would be required to do so. Many doctors and hospitals would have to affiliate with health plans. Perhaps most important, employees would probably have to choose different health plans than they already had, and thus change doctors and hospitals.[43] This was the deepest political flaw in Clinton's proposal, and Obama learned from it.

One Republican alternative to Clinton's plan was the Dole-Chafee bill, which required all employers to offer employees coverage, provided vouchers for low-income people who were not eligible for Medicaid, and—important in light of subsequent events—included a mandate for everyone to carry coverage.[44] Dole-Chafee was soon replaced by the Dole-Packwood bill, which provided subsidies for low-income families and limited exclusions for preexisting conditions. Without a mandate, this would have been difficult for insurers to cope with.[45] But in the end, it was not seriously pursued because Republican strategists, led by William Kristol and Representative Newt Gingrich, calculated that it would be better for them politically not to negotiate with Clinton at all. Enactment of the health care bill, Kristol wrote in a widely circulated memo, "will revive the reputation of the party that spends and regulates, the Democrats, as the generous protector of middle-class interests."[46] It became clear to Senate majority leader Robert Dole that if he pursued compromise, he would lose the Republican presidential nomination. "All the cosponsors of Dole-Packwood were prepared to vote against Dole-Packwood," Republican senator Bob Bennett observed, "including Dole and Packwood!"[47] Clinton did not anticipate that the Republicans would be unwilling to make any deal. His defeat on health care gave Republicans a huge boost in the 1994 midterm elections. Democrats lost fifty-four seats in the House and ten in the Senate, and Gingrich became House Speaker. The lesson of this episode, for Republicans, was to oppose health reform not on the merits but just to deny the Democrats a victory. That experience shaped the Republican response to Obama.

George W. Bush made no effort to bring about universal insurance, but he did preside over an immense expansion of Medicare, adding prescription drug coverage (and financing it entirely with added debt). His strategy also had lessons for Obama. Bush bargained with each of the most important stakeholders, blunting opposition. Unlike Clinton, he did not try to cut costs while creating a new entitlement. He let Congress work out the details.[48]

Bush's interest in health care was, however, confined to expanding benefits for senior citizens, a powerful voting bloc. He repeatedly vetoed bipartisan legislation to expand the State Children's Health Insurance Program.[49] For the uninsured, all he had to offer was tax credits for purchasing insurance (which were too small to help much and in any case were no comfort to those with preexisting conditions) and reform of medical malpractice laws (which have nothing to do with declining coverage). Even Bush's own economists did not think his proposals would extend coverage to more than a small fraction of the uninsured.[50]

OBAMA

When Barack Obama took office, the American health care system did a fine job of delivering care to some Americans, and a terrible job with many others. Those in the first group, the ones who were well taken care of, primarily included workers who got good insurance from their employers, and retirees on Medicare. The losers were those in jobs that did not provide insurance, small-business owners, independent contractors who needed to purchase their insurance in the nongroup markets, and the unemployed.

At the same time, under the pressure of rising costs, the group with employer health insurance was shrinking. From 2000 to 2006, family health coverage premiums rose 87%, in a period with cumulative inflation of 18% and cumulative wage growth of 20%. Most of that wage growth was at the top of the scale;

median household income declined by nearly 3%.[51] From 2000 to 2006, the percentage of firms that offered health insurance dropped from 69% to 61%, and as we saw in the introduction, the fall was concentrated among the worst-paid workers.[52] Low health insurance premiums and tight labor markets had once induced employers to provide coverage for their workers. Now high premiums and high unemployment created pressure in the opposite direction. By the 1990s, the most successful corporations were those like Wal-Mart, which offered minimal benefits and restricted them to full-time workers who had been employed by the company for at least two years. In 2005, less than half of Wal-Mart's employees had company-sponsored insurance.[53] In the markets for individual coverage and small businesses, younger and healthier people were going without coverage (increasing numbers of those with jobs could not afford their share of the premiums), with a serious danger of a "death spiral" in which more and more people elect to go without insurance and the insurance market collapses for want of a sufficiently large pool.

Obama's experts concluded that without expanded coverage, it would be impossible to control costs. Big insurers and providers had no incentive to devise cost-saving innovations as long as they could rely on the more familiar avenue of weeding out the frail and sick.[54]

The reforms that had been adopted in the past made it harder to adopt any new ones in the future. The system of employer-provided insurance conceals its real costs from its beneficiaries. Employees think that some of the funding comes from their employers, even though economists have shown that any employer contribution reduces wages. Targeted programs cover the elderly and veterans, who are well organized and sympathetic, and who feel that (unlike other claimants) they have earned their benefits. (The "tea party" consisted mainly of older white people who already had protection and did not want to pay for anyone else's.)[55] A rich health care industry does not want to jeopardize its privileges. Because most people are satisfied, the system is difficult to change.[56] Given the formidable barriers, the passage of such ambitious legislation is an impressive accomplishment.

A promising, and then-bipartisan, solution had been adopted in 2005 by Massachusetts, under its Republican governor, Mitt Romney (with the active collaboration of Edward Kennedy, who made sure that federal support was available). Massachusetts faced the same problem as every other state: a large majority who were happy with their insurance coverage, and a minority who lacked adequate health insurance, either because they could not afford it or because preexisting conditions made it impossible for them to get it. A different redistributive strategy was necessary for each group. The ones who could not afford it could be subsidized. But subsidies for those with preexisting conditions would be unsustainably large, so regulation was also necessary.

The Massachusetts solution has three prongs, each of which was duplicated by the ACA. The first is to ban insurers from discriminating against applicants with preexisting conditions, or from canceling policies after people get sick. The second is to require everyone to have insurance, thereby putting everyone in the same pool. The third is subsidies for those too poor to pay the full cost of their insurance. Less than 3% of the Massachusetts population was uninsured by 2008, compared with 14% before implementation.[57]

Obama's basic strategy was to expand coverage for the uninsured while delicately navigating around any interference with existing arrangements. The ACA is complex, and it would take a book to adequately describe it.[58] The basic outline, however, is straightforward. Medicaid is henceforth to be available to everyone with an income below 138% of the poverty level (133%, which is the number the Supreme Court would later cite, plus a 5% "income disregard" that ignores that much of a person's income in determining eligibility), adding 18 million people to the rolls. (This is the one provision that was thrown into doubt by the Supreme Court's decision, which declared that states were at liberty to reject the money.) Businesses with more than fifty employees must provide insurance or pay a penalty. Qualifying small businesses get a subsidy in the first two years they provide insurance. Tax credits to subsidize insurance are given to individuals earning between 100 and 400% of the poverty level. Insurance exchanges are created to make insurance more accessible and affordable in the individual and small group markets.

The law is one of the most redistributive in American history. The Medicaid expansion is a huge benefit to the working poor. The subsidies are financed by an increase in the Medicare withholding tax for individuals earning over $200,000 or families earning over $250,000. An estimated 74% of the proceeds will come from households earning over $1 million, and 91% from households earning over $500,000. Only about 2.6% of households will pay the higher tax. The other 97% have no tax increase. Most of the benefit accrues to the poor and uninsured.[59] When subsidies are accounted for, the Congressional Budget Office (CBO) estimates that the average cost of buying insurance in the individual market will fall by almost 60% by 2016, and the cost for small groups such as small businesses will drop by about 10%.[60] Because of new revenue and cost savings, the CBO estimated that the ACA would reduce the federal deficit by $143 billion in the first ten years.[61] On the other hand, the law is only a first step toward decent universal health care. The limited insurance that everyone is required to carry has such high deductibles and coinsurance that financial hardship as a consequence of illness remains a real possibility for many.[62]

The health reform statute responds to the problem of preexisting conditions in two ways. The guaranteed issue requirement bars denying coverage to those with preexisting conditions. The community rating requirement prohibits insurers from charging much higher rates to people based on their medical history.[63] The law also bans "rescission," the practice of canceling an insurance policy after the policyholder becomes sick.

This would enormously ameliorate the lives of millions of people. But it carries with it a danger: they can wait until they get sick before they insure themselves. That, we have already seen, would unravel insurance markets. The mandate is a solution to that problem.

It was well understood that the mandate would not be politically popular. It was adopted because there were no other options left for universal coverage. It was politically impossible to universalize a government health service, like the Veterans Administration, or single-payer health insurance, like Medicare. Blue Cross and charitable hospitals had voluntarily tried to provide low-cost coverage to those with preexisting conditions, and pass on the costs to their healthy customers. But you can't do that in a free market, because competitors will lure the healthy customers away. Government mandates for cross-subsidization, such as the Hill-Burton program and required access to emergency rooms, could not do the job, because hospitals don't have enough resources to take care of everyone. Incentives for employer-provided insurance already existed and got stronger with the ACA, but they are no help to the unemployed and may be a crushing burden for small businesses.

As is now well known, the mandate was originally a conservative idea, calculated to forestall more statist Democratic proposals. It was first put forth in a 1989 paper by Stuart Butler of the Heritage Foundation, and again two years later by economist

Mark Pauly and his colleagues.[64] These in turn became the basis of the ephemeral Dole-Chafee proposal, the Republican alternative to Clinton's employer mandate. (Clinton's plan also included penalties for failing to insure, but almost no one noticed.)

The conservative case for the mandate was laid out in a 1994 article by Robert E. Moffitt of the Heritage Foundation. Because everyone already has to pay for the uninsured, through taxes and higher medical bills, "we already have a mandate." Some people will "take advantage of their fellow citizens by not protecting themselves or their families, with the full knowledge that if they do incur a catastrophic illness...we will, after all is said and done, take care of them and pay all of the bills. They will be correct in this assessment. But the rest of us should realize that we are thus being victimized by deliberate irresponsibility."[65] Among those later challenging the mandate were persons who claimed, with a perfectly straight face, that they did not use health care services and never would. (There are hardly any such people. A survey of uninsured nonelderly adult Americans found that 1% reported "no need for insurance," while most cited the high cost (54%) or job-related reasons such as loss of employment (41%).[66]) As Moffitt observed, they will change their tune if they get sick. Mitt Romney observed: "It's the ultimate conservative idea, which is that people have responsibility for their own care, and they don't look to government...if they can afford to take care of themselves."[67]

In the 2007–08 Democratic primaries, all the Democratic presidential candidates had health care plans—John Edwards deserves credit for going first, with a plan much like the one that was eventually enacted, and so forcing his opponents (including Obama) to commit to their own specifics—but they disagreed about how to implement it. Obama capitalized on his opposition to a health care mandate, which Hillary Clinton supported. A February 2008 Obama mailer warned: "[T]he way Hillary Clinton's health care plan covers everyone is to have the government force uninsured people to buy insurance, even if they can't afford it.... Punishing families who can't afford health care to begin with just *doesn't make sense*." It reinforced Obama's image as more easygoing, less bossy than Clinton.[68] At the same time, Obama never offered any alternative policy that would avoid unraveling insurance markets if preexisting conditions were protected. It's not clear whether he was irresponsibly exploiting the unpopularity of an unavoidable policy, or if he just didn't yet see the necessity of a mandate. Tinkerbell is not necessarily a Republican.

Soon after Obama had secured the nomination, the president of American Health Insurance Plans visited his campaign headquarters to tell him that a mandate was the price of the industry's cooperation.[69] By July 2008, when a staff member asked him what he thought of the mandate, Obama told her, "I kind of think Hillary was right."[70]

The mandate was never an issue in the general election, and it became the assumed policy in the White House. A former Hillary Clinton staffer, Nancy-Anne DeParle, persuaded Obama in April 2009 that without the mandate, 28 million would remain uninsured, while the mandate would reduce that number to less than 10 million.[71]

Because Congress took the lead on writing legislation, Obama never needed to publicly reverse himself. Every bill that came out of the Senate and House committees included a mandate. Opponents focused on other issues: abortion, coverage of illegal immigrants, whether there would be a public option for insurance. Republicans were not much troubled. Senator Charles Grassley said in June 2009, "I believe that there is a bipartisan consensus to have individual mandates." (He later changed his mind.) Legal experts told Democrats there was no case against a mandate's constitutionality.

A few months later, the Republicans abandoned the mandate, and soon after that, they all agreed it was unconstitutional. But this was because they had also abandoned the idea of universal health coverage. Their central proposals were allowing insurance to be sold across state lines, which would have meant that the least-regulated state would dominate the market and thus effectively end all insurance regulation, and limits on medical malpractice lawsuits, which would reduce American health care spending by about half of 1%.[72] Neither would have much effect on the number of uninsured. Tough Luck Libertarianism had prevailed within the Republican Party. The Democrats reasonably concluded that it was impossible to work with Republicans on health care reform. Any bipartisan agreement would have required Democrats to become Tough Luck Libertarians as well.[73]

The mandate's inclusion in the law was assured by a CBO report indicating that eliminating it would raise the uninsured population in 2019 by 16 million, with insurance rates rising by 15 to 20% for those who bought insurance individually.[74]

The provision itself was drafted somewhat differently in the House and Senate versions of the bill. The House bill levied 2.5% of a taxpayer's income and labeled it a "tax on individuals without acceptable health care coverage,"[75] while the Senate version, which is the one finally enacted, called it a "shared responsibility payment."[76] Although there was no ambiguity about how the law operated, some senators evidently didn't want to admit that they were voting for a tax. Hardly anyone imagined that the difference in labels could make a constitutional difference.

One of the principal complaints against the ACA focused on the special favor it supposedly gave to a powerful interest group: here, the insurance companies that everyone was to be forced to contract with. Many who raised this objection would not have had the same complaint about a single-payer system, which would not have given private actors a permanent claim on their fellow citizens. Supporters of the ACA typically responded that they didn't love the insurance companies either, but that there was no hope of enacting health care reform without the cooperation of these powerful stakeholders. The insurance companies themselves argued, with some justice, that if they were required to insure the sick, they needed some compensating expansion of the pool.

The "mandate" isn't really a mandate. In Switzerland or Japan, if the government finds out that you're not carrying insurance, you're enrolled automatically and sent a bill.[77] The ACA penalty doesn't force you to buy insurance, but it is intended to sting you if you don't. In the Senate Finance Committee in October 2009, the amount of the penalty was lowered significantly, leading worried insurers to release analyses predicting an explosion of premiums. It was raised again in the law as enacted, when higher penalties were necessary in order to get the CBO to conclude that at least 95% of Americans would be covered.[78]

In the ACA as finally enacted, beginning in 2014, every citizen and legal immigrant must have minimal health insurance or pay a penalty. The annual penalty rises until 2016. After that the amount can vary with family size and income level, but the maximum a family is required to pay is the annual premium cost for a minimally adequate insurance plan, 2.5 percent of income, or $2085 (the latter subject to cost-of-living adjustments). There is a large collection of exemptions: undocumented aliens, incarcerated persons, people with religious objections, members of health care sharing ministries, persons with incomes below the tax return filing limit, persons who cannot find the cheapest policy for 8% or less of their income, people uninsured for three months or less, Native Americans, people who would incur a hardship (with administrators given considerable discretion to define that class), and Americans living abroad.

There were alternative policies. Obama thought, during the campaign, that people go without insurance because they can't afford it, and there's some evidence that he was right. The ACA's subsidies would have reduced the number of uninsured even without the mandate. Congress could have automatically enrolled individuals as a default but let them opt out, or imposed limited open-enrollment periods with penalties for late enrollment. An analysis of these options found that none of them would cover more than two-thirds as many of the uninsured as the ACA, none saves as much money, and all of them involve higher insurance costs.[79] There is, of course, no way to be sure, and no way to know in advance whether the penalty is strong enough to avoid the adverse selection problem. It may need to be recalibrated. (This is one problem with the Supreme Court dissenters' view that invalidating the mandate would necessarily unravel the whole statute.) Everyone is guessing based on speculative models. But the states' experience showed that some compulsory expansion of coverage is indispensable.

You may not like the mandate. It may not have been worth the political cost, and it nearly killed the whole law. But without it, millions more people will be uninsured. If you abandon the mandate, you probably abandon near-universal health care.

TWO

Appropriate Constitutional Limits

Does Congress have the power to enact the mandate? In order to answer this question, we need to step back and think more broadly about the powers of Congress under the Constitution. In order to assess those powers, we need to step back still further, and ask why the Constitution exists at all.

The objection to the mandate is driven, at its root, by the conviction that the federal government has gotten too big, and that its power must somehow be contained. This concern is often coupled with the observation that the framers of the Constitution never imagined the huge and elaborate federal bureaucracy that now exists. The modern administrative state is thus one of the prime targets of "originalism," the movement to make constitutional law conform with the original meaning of the text. We should begin, then, by considering whether, if we aim to read the Constitution faithfully, there is some deep problem with the present regime, so that some kind of new limitation is necessary.

THE ENUMERATED POWERS

It is true that the framers did not anticipate far-reaching federal regulatory schemes such as the ACA. However, there can be a tension between specific and more general intentions. Suppose you are a theater director presenting Shakespeare's *Romeo and Juliet*. Here's a simple-sounding question: Are you legitimately interpreting what Shakespeare wrote if you cast a female performer as Juliet? It may sound silly, but Shakespeare wrote the play for his own company, and he clearly intended that Juliet be played by a teenage boy, since females were not permitted to act on the Elizabethan stage. The script of a play is like a recipe: it relies on publicly shared assumptions about the character of the ingredients.[1] "Flour" refers to ground kernels of wheat, and "Juliet" refers to a boy costumed as a girl. Given modern conventions, this creates a dilemma for the director. You can stage the play exactly the way Shakespeare imagined you would, but the male Juliet will distract the audience from the story you're trying to tell. Or you can cast a female Juliet, in which case you will be disregarding Shakespeare's specific intentions—or, as some originalists would put it, the public meaning of his script—in order to realize his most general purpose, which is to tell this story in a convincing way. (Even with recipes, you sometimes must vary the proportions when baking at a high elevation.) Shakespeare did not foresee all the changes in theatrical conventions that have occurred since he wrote his play. Those changed circumstances are good reasons to modify performance practices. Such modification is not merely *consistent* with faithful interpretation. It may be demanded by it.

The Constitution was adopted specifically to give Congress power adequate to address the nation's problems. That is its fundamental and overriding purpose, in the same way that Shakespeare's fundamental and overriding purpose was to move audiences to tears. A situation in which neither the states nor the federal government had adequate power to address the country's problems was precisely what the Constitution was intended to prevent. Critics of the modern administrative state are right that the framers never imagined such a large government. But they are right in the same way that it is right that Shakespeare never imagined a female Juliet.

Under the Articles of Confederation, states interposed tariff barriers at their borders, strangling commerce in this new and poor nation. Congress couldn't levy taxes but had to request funds from the states, whose reluctance to contribute their share meant that federal finances were increasingly dire. That meant a weak military in a world full of foreign enemies.

So the Constitution created a more powerful government, with these and many other powers. It also, significantly, created a different *kind* of government: not merely a league of independent sovereignties but a nation. America's bad experience with the British monarchy, however, called for three kinds of limits: division of power between the national and state governments (a division that is generally referred to by the shorthand term "federalism"), separation of powers, and the guarantee of individual rights.

What, specifically, does the Constitution empower Congress to do? At Philadelphia in 1787, the Convention resolved that Congress could "legislate in all cases...to which the States are separately incompetent, or in which the harmony of the United States may be interrupted by the exercise of individual legislation."[2] This was then translated by the Committee of Detail into the present enumeration of powers in Article I, Section 8, which was accepted as a functional equivalent by the Convention without much discussion.

The idea that Congress should legislate only when the states can't do it separately is what political philosophers call the principle of *subsidiarity*. It holds that "central authority should have a subsidiary function, performing only those tasks which cannot be performed at a more immediate or local level."[3] Decisions by distant bureaucrats have obvious disadvantages compared with local communities. It is good for people to make decisions over their own lives, in relatively small groups. Different localities have different preferences, and local control accommodates this diversity. States also compete with one another to attract new citizens, and can experiment with new social policies. Such competition also forces states to be more responsive to the needs and preferences of their own citizens, who are free to leave. Sometimes, however, local control will leave problems unsolved. Interstate competition can sometimes produce a "race to the bottom" in which policies that almost no one wants—protective tariffs at state borders and refusal to contribute to the federal budget were the examples that motivated the framers—gives a competitive advantage to states that pursue them. That was what was wrong with the Articles of Confederation. Subsidiarity requires the center to act when local bodies cannot do so.[4]

Did the Committee of Detail botch its job, creating a regime in which Congress could not legislate in some of the cases the separate states were incompetent to address? Did the Convention not notice the change? No. "[T]he purpose of enumeration," Jack Balkin observes, "was not to *displace* the principle but to *enact* it."[5]

Most of the enumerated powers are clear and limited. Some are quite potent, such as the general "Power To lay and collect Taxes," which eventually became the basis for the Court's decision to uphold the ACA. Under the taxing power, Congress can make any activity prohibitively expensive. The Court held that the mandate was an exercise of the taxing power. There is also the spending power, "to pay the Debts and provide for the common Defence and general Welfare of the United States." With this authority, Congress has offered states powerful financial inducements to participate in federal programs, most notably Medicaid, through which billions are distributed to the states. That was the basis of the enormous Medicaid expansion.

The power that has tended to expand the most is that "to regulate Commerce . . . among the several States." It was the focus of the constitutional debate on the ACA, even though the tax power turned out to be what saved the law.

Originalists have furiously debated the meaning of the word "commerce" at the time of the framing. Randy Barnett, who we shall see was the main intellectual force behind the constitutional challenge to the ACA, argues that it meant only trade and transportation, but not manufacturing or agriculture. Balkin offers evidence that it referred to all interaction between people.[6] I will not try to adjudicate the linguistic debate here, but I will observe that it at least shows that the contemporaneous use of the term is ambiguous. Balkin's reading is more consistent with the overall purpose and history of the Constitution.

The best reading of the power to regulate commerce "among the several States" is that it authorizes Congress to regulate, as Chief Justice Marshall put it, "commerce which concerns more States than one"—that has interstate spillover effects, or that generates collective action problems that no state can solve alone.[7] The germinal work here is that of Robert Stern, who observed in 1934 that the framers did not intend for some commerce to be uncontrollable by either the state or the federal governments, nor that the people of the United States "be entirely unable to help themselves through any existing social or governmental agency."[8]

That view was not uncontroversial at the time of the framing. Some Americans thought that the Constitution created too powerful a government, and that it would be better to retain the weak articles. They were the Antifederalists, the party that sought to block ratification of the Constitution, and they came within a few votes of succeeding. They had no good account of how to deal with interstate problems, however, and when you read them today their arguments feel delusional. Their concerns were addressed to some extent by the early addition of the Bill of Rights.

The Constitution should not be read as if the Antifederalists had won.

Yet that is the position that the four dissenters took in the ACA case. Here is their argument:

> The Constitution…enumerates not federally soluble *problems*, but federally available *powers*. The Federal Government can address whatever problems it wants but can bring to their solution only those powers that the Constitution confers, among which is the power to regulate commerce. None of our cases say anything else. Article I contains no whatever-it-takes-to-solve-a-national-problem power.

It follows that there are some national problems that no one can solve, even though no author of the Constitution ever intended that they remain unsolved. That reading might have to be adopted if there is no other way to interpret the pertinent text, but there is enough ambiguity and room for construction of "commerce" that the term can and should be read in a way that is not at war with the Constitution's larger purposes.

Thus far our inquiry has been purely originalist, and has assumed that the Constitution should be read solely according to the original public meaning of its language. This is, however, a potentially catastrophic approach to constitutional interpretation.

It means that, if new research shows that the original semantic meaning is different than we had previously thought, then we must upend our legal system in response. At least until the next bit of historical research comes along: if some later scholar shows us that the first one was wrong, then we lurch back to the law we had before. Large federal programs may disappear and reappear, depending on the state of the latest scholarship. This would be an insane way to run a civilization. In considering originalist proposals to radically reshape American constitutional law, one should not ignore the enormous success of the American regime, and the flourishing of individual freedom therein.

In the first paragraph of the *Federalist Papers*, Alexander Hamilton wrote: "It has been frequently remarked that it seems to have been reserved to the people of this country, by their conduct and example, to decide the important question, whether societies of men are really capable or not of establishing good government from reflection and choice, or whether they are forever destined to depend for their political constitutions on accident and force." If the dissenters are correct, then accident is what shapes the fate of contemporary Americans, and Hamilton's aspiration is a failure. The Constitution enumerates the powers that were thought necessary in the 1800s. If there are Americans who will die today unless the federal government exercises powers that were omitted from that list, then die they must. This is not because the framers thought this a just result. It is because we are caught by the limits of their foresight. They left some powers off their list that turn out to be important, and they compounded the injury by making the Constitution extremely hard to amend (as it happens, harder than any other constitution in the world).[9] It is just our tough luck that we are imprisoned by these limitations. We live under a tough luck Constitution.

NECESSARY AND PROPER

The commerce power is the source of Congress's ability to regulate the insurance industry. We shall shortly consider whether it has been appropriate to read it that way. First, however, we must introduce another pertinent constitutional provision. The list of congressional powers in Article I ends with an authorization to "make all Laws which shall be necessary and proper" to carry out its responsibilities.[10]

The Necessary and Proper Clause was always the principal obstacle to the constitutional challenge to the ACA. The challengers rarely questioned Congress's power to forbid insurers from turning away sick people. Instead, they argued that the mandate was an improper means for carrying out this purpose. In making that claim, they had to navigate around nearly two centuries of settled law. They never did figure out how to do that, and, as we shall see, Chief Justice Roberts's approval of their Commerce Clause challenge was opaque on this central question.

The interpretation of the Necessary and Proper Clause was settled in 1819 by Chief Justice John Marshall in *McCulloch v. Maryland*.[11] The central question in *McCulloch* was whether Congress had the power to charter the Bank of the United States, the precursor of today's Federal Reserve Bank. The Constitution does not enumerate any power to create corporations. The state of Maryland, which was trying to tax the Bank, argued that the "necessary and proper" language permitted Congress only to choose means that were *absolutely* necessary to carry out those powers. The same view was taken by Thomas Jefferson, who feared a government possessing "a boundless field of power, no longer susceptible of any definition."[12]

Marshall rejected this reading, which, he thought, would make the government "incompetent to its great objects." The federal government must collect and spend revenue through-out the United States, and so must quickly transfer funds across hundreds of miles. "Is that construction of the constitution to be preferred which would render these operations hazardous, diffi-cult, and expensive?" Without implied powers, Marshall argued, Congress's power "to establish post offices" could not entail the ability to punish mail robbers and might not even entail the power to carry letters from one post office to another. "It may be said with some plausibility that the right to carry the mail, and to punish those who rob it, is not indispensably necessary to the establishment of a post office and post road." He concluded that Congress could choose any convenient means for carrying out its enumerated powers.

So Congress is powerful—perhaps frighteningly powerful. But what Marshall said about the taxing power is true of the other powers as well: "The only security against the abuse of this power is found in the structure of the Government itself. In imposing a tax, the legislature acts upon its constituents. This is, in gen-eral, a sufficient security against erroneous and oppressive taxa-tion." The political accountability that Marshall emphasizes here is another reason why it makes sense to give Congress a choice of means. Opponents of the mandate sometimes suggest that it's rep-rehensible that Congress allowed political considerations to shape the law and eliminate options such as single-payer. But taking account of politics is Congress's job. The various possible means for addressing any problem are likely to affect different people differently, and those who are going to suffer if one or the other choice is made should have the opportunity to have that taken into account. That's democracy.

The basic rule of *McCulloch* was reaffirmed by the Court as recently as May 2010 in *United States v. Comstock*.[13] The Court upheld a law authorizing civil commitment of mentally ill sexual predators who remain dangerous after completing their federal prison sentences—an appropriate federal role, Congress found, because no state may be willing to take custody, and the federal imprisonment had created that problem. (The Court did not address the obvious individual rights issue, which was litigated separately.) In deciding whether Congress is appropriately exercising its powers under the Necessary and Proper Clause, the Court declared, the question is "whether the statute constitutes a means that is rationally related to the implementation of a constitutionally enumerated power." Thus, for example, even though the Constitution mentions no federal crimes other than counterfeiting, treason, and piracy, Congress has broad authority to enact criminal statutes.

Congress's powers are broad but not infinite. The federal government is one of limited and enumerated powers, and as Marshall observed, "[t]he enumeration presupposes something not enumerated."[14] The most sensible limitation, the one originally intended, is the principle of subsidiarity. Of course, it does not follow that this principle should be judicially enforced. That depends on several things: the competence of the judiciary, and what is likely to happen absent judicial enforcement. Both of those questions can only be answered by considering the historical record.

THE UNHAPPY STORY OF JUDICIALLY CRAFTED LIMITS

Throughout American history, when courts have tried to craft limits on congressional power, they have botched it.

The limits of federal power were not much tested in the courts until after the Civil War. Then began a new and troubling pattern, of construing congressional power in an arbitrarily narrow way, without regard to its purposes. There have been two major Supreme Court interventions: against Reconstruction, and against economic regulation of the economy until the 1930s. In each case, the Court said it was protecting liberty by restraining the federal government. In each case, it removed federal restraints on abusive private power, so that the abuses continued for decades. This is not a happy story for liberty.

Begin with Reconstruction. After the Civil War, the Thirteenth Amendment abolished slavery. The Fourteenth, which forbade the states from denying "the equal protection of the laws," was adopted with the specific purpose of invalidating the "Black Codes" that had been adopted by white-controlled Southern legislatures after Appomattox. The codes imposed specific legal disabilities on blacks, such as requiring them to be gainfully employed under contracts of long duration, excluding them from occupations other than manual labor, and disabling them from testifying against whites in court. The Fifteenth forbade states from denying the right to vote on the basis of "race, color, or previous condition of servitude." The central purpose of the Civil War Amendments was to guarantee the equal citizenship of the former slaves.

The promise of the amendments was quickly betrayed, and the Supreme Court helped make that happen. All three amendments gave Congress the power to enforce them, and the framers understood the by then well-established *McCulloch* precedent to give Congress a broad choice of means. The former Confederates, now organized into a new terrorist organization called the Ku Klux Klan, violently resisted black equality. Congress responded by enacting a series of civil rights and antilynching laws, and the Justice Department used these to prosecute discriminators and terrorists.

In a series of poorly reasoned decisions, the Supreme Court repeatedly invalidated these statutes on technical grounds, and radically narrowed the scope of the amendments, all in the name of federalism and states' rights. The amendments plainly gave citizens new rights against state governments, but the Court thought they could not possibly mean what they said, because this would "fetter and degrade the State governments by subjecting them to the control of Congress." The Court could not imagine that the Fourteenth Amendment "radically changes the whole theory of the relations of the State and Federal governments to each other and of both these governments to the people."[15] Justice Stephen Field, dissenting, observed that under the majority's reading, the amendment "was a vain and idle enactment, which accomplished nothing, and most unnecessarily excited Congress and the people on its passage."

United States v. Cruikshank[16] involved a federal prosecution of members of a white militia after the "Colfax massacre," in which dozens of blacks had been slaughtered after an election dispute turned violent. The Court set the killers free, invalidating the Enforcement Act of 1870, which made it a felony for two or more people to conspire to deprive anyone of his constitutional rights. "The fourteenth amendment prohibits a State from depriving any person of life, liberty, or property, without due process of law; but this adds nothing to the rights of one citizen as against another." Therefore, there was no constitutional violation for Congress to act against. One white Southern lawyer described the reaction to the decision in Louisiana as "the utmost joy...and with it a return of confidence which gave best hopes for the future."[17] Historian Leonard Levy writes that "*Cruikshank* paralyzed the federal government's attempt to protect black citizens by punishing violators of their Civil Rights and, in effect, shaped the Constitution to the advantage of the Ku Klux Klan."[18]

Reconstruction was long past in 1905, but the U.S. Justice Department still sometimes would prosecute abuses against blacks. In *Hodges v. United States*,[19] the Court struck down the Civil Rights

Act of 1866, which made it a crime to conspire to deprive anyone of their constitutional rights, such as the right to make contracts. The defendants were white men who had used violence and threats to force African American workers to leave their jobs at a sawmill. The Court said that the Reconstruction Amendments "declined to constitute them wards of the nation...doubtless believing that thereby, in the long run, their best interests would be subserved, they taking their chances with other citizens in the states where they should make their homes." Pamela Karlan observes that the *Hodges* Court—in 1906!—"viewed the problems of blacks as already solved."[20]

The Court did allow federal intervention if the federal government could prove that states failed to protect rights, and federal authorities did use that power, at least when Republicans held the presidency.[21] But the Court's niggling reading of the Constitution hampered those efforts, not least by prominently freeing white murderers. The Court thought it was promoting liberty, but in fact, by disabling Big Government, it helped bring about the worst oppression of American citizens in our history.

The Court lectured Congress on the need to rewrite its statutes to comport with these newly devised constitutional limitations. No rewriting occurred. The political moment had passed, and there was no more federal civil rights legislation until 1957. This episode has obvious analogies with the ACA litigation. Given the enormous difficulty of passing this statute, the chances of another universal health care law in the near future, had the Court invalidated it, were approximately nil.

The Court was not much troubled by racist legislation, upholding a racial segregation law in the now-notorious *Plessy v. Ferguson*, but it was sometimes aggressive in protecting economic liberties. This had implications for congressional power, but they were indirect.

In cases typified by *Lochner v. New York*,[22] the Court sometimes struck down state-level labor legislation. *Lochner* itself threw out a maximum-hours law for bakers. The Court upheld more laws than it invalidated, but the labor movement could never feel sure that major legislative reform, such as the New York law, would survive judicial review. These cases all involved state laws, but they had the effect of limiting possibilities for federal action. Historians have puzzled for a long time about why there has been no organized working-class political party in the United States, as there has been in most other advanced industrial countries. The unusually strong American judiciary is an important part of the answer: judicial intervention made collective political action risky here. Law was abandoned as an instrument of social transformation, and instead labor attempted to win gains through collective bargaining on an industry-by-industry basis, with victories predictably concentrated among the most skilled workers in key, bottleneck industries such as coal, steel, and automobiles.[23] So fewer and fewer workers belonged to unions, and those who didn't had little sympathy for the labor movement, which, they thought, benefited only a privileged few. Germany adopted the first national health care law in order to take the issue away from the Left. In America, there was no powerful party of the Left to provoke such countermeasures.

One implication of *Lochner*-style jurisprudence is that government redistribution is absolutely forbidden. An Ohio court in 1906 struck down an act providing relief for the blind, declaring that such a law created a dangerous precedent: "If a bounty may be conferred upon individuals of one class, then it may be upon individuals of another class...innumerable classes may clamor for similar bounties...and it is doubted that any line could be drawn short of an equal distribution of property."[24] The Supreme Court later declared, anticipating Tough Luck Libertarianism, that "it is from the nature of things impossible to uphold freedom of contract and the right of private property without at the same time recognizing as legitimate those inequalities of fortune that are the necessary result of the exercise of those rights."[25]

Resistance to redistribution also played a role in the Court's extraordinary 1895 decision to invalidate the federal income tax. That decision was overruled in 1913 by the Sixteenth Amendment. It was no longer possible to argue that the existing distribution of property is constitutionally sacrosanct, because everyone understood that the amendment authorized progressive taxation.

The late nineteenth century was also the period when the federal government for the first time attempted to regulate the national economy. The Court responded by laying down stringent limitations on the more open-ended grants of power to Congress.

In *United States v. E. C. Knight* (1895), the Court invalidated the application of the Sherman Antitrust Act to the Sugar Trust (an entity that survives today as Domino Sugar), which controlled 98% of the sugar-refining market. "Commerce succeeds to manufacture, and is not part of it. The fact that an article is manufactured for export to another state does not itself make it an article of interstate commerce." Justice John Marshall Harlan, dissenting, thought that if there were anything that "affects commerce" that the states couldn't competently regulate, the federal government had to have the power to do it:

> The common government of all the people is the only one that can adequately deal with a matter which directly and injuriously affects the entire commerce of the country, which concerns equally all the people of the Union, and which, it must be confessed, cannot be adequately

controlled by any one state. Its authority should not be so weakened by construction that it cannot reach and eradicate evils that, beyond all question, tend to defeat an object which that government is entitled, by the constitution, to accomplish.

Harlan's reasoning here is identical with that of the framers at the Constitutional Convention.

The Court devised an elaborate set of limitations on congressional power: commerce included only trade and navigation; Congress could regulate actions that affected commerce directly, but not indirectly; trade, but not manufacturing, mining, or agriculture; it could not even regulate what crossed state lines if its purpose was to affect intrastate activities. These judge-made categories were crafted for the sake of limiting government power. They promoted Tough Luck Libertarianism.

Child labor was the issue that made those limitations salient. Like the ACA, child labor legislation was the product of a decades-long struggle. The movement to abolish child labor started after the Civil War: when the Knights of Labor was founded in 1869, its constitution included a provision calling for abolition of child labor, and a similar position was adopted by the new American Federation of Labor in 1886.[26] The National Child Labor Committee was organized in 1904, and the first federal bill was introduced in 1906. President Theodore Roosevelt supported a federal study of the child labor problem. But the bill faced substantial opposition from the Deep South, where the textile industry feared losing its competitive advantage if child labor were outlawed.[27]

Only the federal government could address the problem. Even states that did not want child labor could not afford to get rid of it if their competitors still had it. Critics of child labor were acutely aware of the collective action problem.[28] In 1916, Congress, using its power to regulate interstate commerce, banned the interstate shipment of the products of child labor, by a margin of 337–46 in the House and 52–12 in the Senate.[29] In the Supreme Court, the government explained that this was an interstate problem: "The shipment of child-made goods outside of one State directly induces similar employment of children in competing states."[30]

Then as now, challengers to the statutes had to devise previously unheard-of constitutional rules. There was nothing in the Supreme Court's case law that suggested any limit on Congress's authority over what crossed state lines. On the contrary, the Court had upheld bans on interstate transportation of lottery tickets, contaminated food and drugs, prostitutes, and alcoholic beverages.

The Supreme Court's invalidation of the law in *Hammer v. Dagenhart* (1918) astounded even those who had most strenuously opposed enactment. The Court declared that if it upheld the law, "all freedom of commerce will be at an end, and the power of the States over local matters may be eliminated, and, thus, our system of government be practically destroyed."[31] Justice Oliver Wendell Holmes, dissenting, wondered how it could make sense for congressional regulation to be "permissible as against strong drink but not as against the product of ruined lives." The Court responded that unlike all the contraband that it had permitted Congress to block, the products of child labor "are of themselves harmless." The Court conferred upon itself the power to decide which harms Congress was permitted to consider when it regulated commerce.

The decision provoked a wave of national revulsion. Congress responded that same year with a second law, a tax on products of child labor. Here, surely, Congress was acting within its rights. The Constitution gives Congress a nearly unlimited power of taxation. But the Court struck down this law, too, in *Bailey v. Drexel Furniture*, which was unashamedly cited by opponents of the health care mandate (who needed to beat back the claim, which ultimately did them in, that the mandate is a valid exercise of the taxing power).[32] "To give such magic to the word 'tax,'" the Court thundered, "would be to break down all constitutional limitation of the powers of Congress and completely wipe out the sovereignty of the States." The problem, the Court explained, was that Congress was trying to regulate manufacturing, which was a matter reserved to the states. Edward Corwin, one of the leading constitutional scholars of the time, noted with astonishment that the decision, "overriding previous decisions, makes the Court the supervisor of the purposes for which Congress may exercise its constitutional powers."[33]

What the Court actually accomplished in 1918 was to thwart democracy and consign large numbers of children to the textile mills for two decades.

The challengers to the law, ordinary folk who were frightened of federal power, should really have feared their "friends" who were trying to shake off government regulation. The prevailing claim in the first Supreme Court child labor case was made by a father whose sons had been working sixty hours per week in a North Carolina factory. He claimed—here, as in the health care case, federal-power claims blended into individual-liberties ones—that the law violated his rights by depriving him of his children's earnings. Several years later, Reuben Dagenhart, one of those boys, reflected on the constitutional rights that the Supreme Court had given him. "We got some automobile rides" from the wealthy businessmen's committee that had financed the litigation. "They bought both of us a Coca-Cola. That's what we got out of it." At age twenty, having worked twelve hours a day since the age of twelve, now with a wife and child, he said:

Look at me! A hundred and five pounds, a grown man and no education. I may be mistaken, but I think the years

I've put in the cotton mills have stunted my growth. They kept me from getting my schooling. I had to stop school after the third grade and now I need the education I didn't get. It would have been a good thing for all the kids in this state if that law they passed had been kept.[34]

All the judicial limitations on congressional power collapsed in the 1930s, when the pressure of economic catastrophe empowered President Roosevelt to undertake unprecedented national regulation. The Court resisted at first, then capitulated. *Hammer* was overruled in 1941.[35] Roosevelt eventually appointed a majority of the justices. After that, for more than half a century, the Court made no attempt to enforce limitations on congressional power. That made possible a huge range of laws that would have been impossible before the New Deal, including Social Security, Medicare, Medicaid, the Civil Rights Act of 1964, the Clean Air and Clean Water Acts, and the rest of the apparatus of the modern administrative state. With them came the decisive abandonment of Tough Luck Libertarianism.

The emblematic New Deal case is *Wickard v. Filburn*,[36] which held that Congress could regulate a farmer's decision to grow wheat, even if the wheat never left his farm. The Agricultural Adjustment Act tried to help struggling farmers during the Great Depression by raising wheat prices. It did that by limiting wheat production, including production of homegrown wheat. Farmer Roscoe Filburn grew his wheat to feed to his own hogs, but if he had not grown it, he would have had to buy wheat on the open market. His actions thus affected the price of wheat. "That [the farmer's] own contribution to the demand for wheat may be trivial by itself is not enough to remove him from the scope of federal regulation where, as here, his contribution, taken together with that of many others similarly situated, is far from trivial."

The Court did not explain who "others similarly situated" are. Many have found this reasoning conclusory and unsatisfying, implying no limits at all on congressional power. By the time I took the bar in 1991, my bar review lecturer[37] advised us that the operative rule was easy to remember: Congress can do anything it wants to under the Commerce Clause.

At the same time, the Court relaxed its constraints on the taxing and spending powers. The trouble with judicial restriction of the taxing power is that all taxes both burden the taxed activity and raise revenues, so there is no principled way to decide if any tax is regulatory or revenue-generating. It is also mysterious why a tax can't have a regulatory purpose. *Drexel* was never formally overruled, but the Court clearly abandoned its holding that the Court would monitor the purposes for which Congress used its tax powers. It was cited intermittently, but just what remained of it was uncertain.

Limits on the spending power likewise disappeared. The rule of the child labor cases, that Congress can't use its general powers of taxing and spending except in pursuit of its enumerated powers, would also have invalidated Social Security, because such social welfare measures were not among the enumerated powers of Congress. But the Court upheld that program and many others.

In 1936, when the constitutionality of Roosevelt's initiatives was one of the central issues in the presidential election, not only was Roosevelt reelected with 60% of the vote, but the Republican caucus was shriveled to sixteen senators and eighty-nine representatives. The voters responded to the constitutional dispute with one of the largest electoral mandates in American history. The New Deal transformation of constitutional law was so dramatic that some scholars regard it as a de facto constitutional amendment. But the Court's shift can also be understood as a democratically legitimated judicial repudiation of the previously established interpretation of enumerated powers—an interpretation that, after all, was not itself part of the Constitution.

Despite the Court's abandonment of these constitutional limits, federalism somehow survived. The Court has repeatedly insisted that Congress could not displace state tort law, contract law, criminal law, or family law,[38] but these pronouncements were dictum (judicial language unnecessary to the decision of a case) because Congress never tried to take over these areas. Congress did not even draft a federal code of corporations or commercial law, which it undoubtedly still has the power to do.

If you care about the actual liberty of human beings, rather than just constraining Congress, the New Deal reforms look like a pretty good deal. Social Security is the most important and enduring New Deal legislation. When it was enacted, most of the elderly lived in some kind of economic dependency, too poor to support themselves.[39] Today 55% of the elderly get more than half of their income from Social Security, and for 33%, it is more than 80% of their income. Those in the middle of the income distribution get 66% of their income from Social Security, compared with 9% from private pensions and 5% from personal assets.[40]

If subsidiarity—the idea that decisions should be made at a local level whenever practically possible—is the appropriate yardstick, then the post-1930 judicial deference to Congress doesn't look all that bad. (It may also be relevant that the New Deal was followed by decades of unprecedented prosperity.) State and local officials have complained about the burden of federal regulation, but they usually just want the programs to be more flexible, with more generous funding.

There is a respectable case for the Court simply declining to enforce subsidiarity. Some other provisions of the Constitution, such as the guarantee to every state of a "Republican form of government," have been deemed nonjusticiable. The key question is whether it is better for the overall constitutional scheme for this or that provision to be enforced by courts or left to the political branches. I am frankly torn. What is clear to me is that any limit had better not cripple the United States as a whole, making it impossible for some problems to be solved by any government agency, state or federal.

Nonetheless, the Court eventually decided that there must be judicially enforced limits to congressional power. It has been trying for nearly twenty years to develop such limits. The project has not gone well.

In 1995 in *United States v. Lopez*,[41] the Court for the first time since 1937 held that a statute exceeded Congress's powers. The statute in *Lopez* was a pretty easy one from the standpoint of subsidiarity, criminalizing possession of handguns near schools—an issue that there was no reason to think that the states couldn't handle.[42] It didn't involve instrumentalities of commerce such as railroads, or the crossing of state lines—both of which, everyone now concedes, Congress can regulate however it wants. The law in *Lopez* scored cheap political points by appearing to address a pressing and difficult problem without contributing anything substantial to its solution. But the Court did not rely on subsidiarity. Instead, it cited three other considerations, none of which make much sense.

First, the *Lopez* Court noted that Congress had made no findings on the regulated activity's impact on the national economy. But this is no constraint at all. It just demands that Congress say the magic words. Section 1501 of the ACA included more than 500 words of findings about the mandate's importance for the regulation of interstate commerce.

Second, the Court thought it important that the activity involved was traditionally subject to state regulation.[43] The "traditional state concern" test was already tried by the Court in 1976, in an effort to decide when to immunize states from federal law.[44] It held that traditional state functions were immune from federal laws such as wage and hours regulations. But it soon discovered that the courts couldn't figure out what counted as a traditional function, and in 1985, it gave up and overruled its earlier decision.[45] If "tradition" was too vague in that context, there is no reason to think it will be more coherent here.

Finally, the *Lopez* Court thought it relevant that Congress was trying to regulate noneconomic activity, and more recently the Court suggested that this might be the crucial distinction.[46] Justice Kennedy, who cast the deciding vote, thought that congressional power over the economy is plenary: "Congress can regulate in the commercial sphere on the assumption that we have a single market and a unified purpose to build a stable national economy."

The attraction of the economic/noneconomic line is that it is at least coherent, unlike the other two. The trouble is that it has nothing to do with subsidiarity. Maybe it makes sense to say that Congress can regulate any economic transaction, since these so often have interstate effects. The Court's language suggests, however, that this might be the test, not only for what is included in the commerce power but also for what is *excluded*. If that were the rule, then Congress would be deprived of authority over such nontrivial matters as the spoliation of the environment or the spread of contagious diseases across state lines.[47] The Court has already suggested on this basis that Congress may not have the power to regulate wetlands that are wholly within a single state.[48]

The Court began with a constricted understanding of commerce as including only trade and navigation, and then accommodated the modern state by stretching the meaning of this understanding and proliferating legal fictions, producing bizarrely formalistic law. An understanding of commerce limited to trade constrains the federal government with no regard for the reasons why federal regulation might be necessary, and thus pointlessly casts doubt on laws governing civil rights, workplace safety, sanitary food, drug safety, and employee rights.[49]

The Rehnquist Court's commerce power decisions, a leading treatise observes, "invite challenges to countless federal laws."[50] What is to be the fate of the Endangered Species Act, or the Clean Water Act? The federal government has been protecting the environment for more than a century, but there is now deep uncertainty about which parts of this regime must be discarded in the name of the new federalism.[51] The doctrine the Court has contemplated either is indeterminate or dictates politically impossible results.

The *Lopez* revolution turned out to be something of a wet firecracker when the Court distinguished it in *Gonzales v. Raich*,[52] upholding a ban on private cultivation of marijuana. Randy Barnett was the attorney who argued against the ban, pressing hard on the economic/noneconomic distinction and asking the Court to make it an absolute limit on Congress's regulatory power. The Court rejected that claim and held that even noneconomic activity could be regulated if the statute as a whole clearly did regulate interstate commerce (here, the drug trade) and regulating the noneconomic activity "was an essential part of the larger regulatory scheme." That suggests that Congress's power gets greater as its regulatory scheme becomes larger and more complex. It's not clear what's left of *Lopez*.

On the other hand, *Raich* declared: "Our case law firmly establishes Congress' power to regulate purely local activities that are part of an economic 'class of activities' that have a substantial effect on interstate commerce." This suggested—and this became crucial in the challenge to the ACA—that in order to defend an exercise of the commerce power, Congress would have to show that whatever it was regulating was part of an economic class of activities. And that meant that it was crucial that the object of regulation was an activity. This became the seed of the activity/inactivity distinction that was central to the challenge to the ACA.

Raich left a crucial ambiguity in the law of the commerce power: what happens if a provision regulates something—say, the failure to purchase insurance—that is not part of an economic class of activities, but that regulation is nonetheless an essential part of a larger regulatory scheme? This is the core of the dispute over the ACA and the Commerce Clause. The opponents of the ACA mandate thought that, if this question is approached with *McCulloch-Comstock* deference to Congress's choice of means, then it follows that there is no limit at all to congressional power. The ACA's supporters thought that the case for the mandate was so compelling that, even if it was in tension with some of the language in *Raich*, there was no sense in constructing this as a new limit on the commerce power—a limit that *Raich* had not expressly declared. That limit has nothing to do either with the purposes for which federal power is being exercised or with the reasons for which anyone would reasonably want to constrain it. It is a limit just for the sake of having a limit.

A clearer standard has been suggested by Justice Clarence Thomas. He wants to return to the old pre–New Deal categories, proposing that "commerce" be understood to include only "selling, buying, and bartering, as well as transporting for these purposes."[53] Congress should therefore be understood to have no power over productive activities such as manufacturing and agriculture.[54] (It is not clear what one should call Thomas's willingness to tear down long-established institutions on the basis of an abstract and untested theory, but "conservatism" seems the wrong label.)[55] The ACA presented a very easy case for him: if Congress has no power to regulate activity that substantially affects interstate commerce (where "commerce" is understood this narrowly), then of course the mandate is unconstitutional.

Thomas's approach suffers from all the difficulties of indeterminacy and perverse results that bedevil many forms of originalism. Thomas is correct that most of the framers envisioned a far smaller central government than the one we (along with every other modern industrialized nation) now have,[56] but his formulation is in tension with the framers' most basic purposes. Thomas's reading was the sort of interpretation that Chief Justice Marshall warned against in *McCulloch* when he wrote that the Constitution does not "attempt to provide, by immutable rules, for exigencies which, if foreseen at all, must have been seen dimly, and which can be best provided for as they occur." To return to our earlier point, Thomas's "originalism" is just like an insistence that Shakespeare's Juliet be played by a teenage boy: correct on details, but missing the larger point.

Thomas's vision also comes accompanied by a crucial proviso:

> Although I might be willing to return to the original understanding, I recognize that many believe that it is too late in the day to undertake a fundamental reexamination of the past 60 years. Consideration of *stare decisis* and reliance interests may convince us that we cannot wipe the slate clean.[57]

His deference to precedent is only partial, however. He is still prepared to use originalism to get rid of those aspects of existing practice that he is satisfied that the country can do without. For example, he is prepared to abandon all enforcement of the ban on state establishments of religion.[58] So originalism, which originally came billed as a doctrine of judicial restraint, in Thomas's hands becomes a recipe for judicial dictatorship: he gets to decide which parts of the modern federal government have to be dismantled.

A CONSTITUTION OF SUBSIDIARITY

Is there a better way? If the appropriate constitutional limit is subsidiarity—Congress should only be able to legislate in cases where the states are separately incompetent—then why not make that the limit of congressional power?

Subsidiarity is a principle that the judiciary is ill-suited to enforce in any but the weakest fashion. Judges cannot decide which topics are apt for decentralization without imposing their own political views on the rest of us.

It is impossible to disentangle the question of an institution's capacities from what we want the institution to do. The fact that an institution tends to make good decisions is good reason to judge it competent. The fact that an institution tends to make bad decisions is good reason to judge it incompetent. (Of course, in both cases we must be able and authorized to distinguish good decisions from bad ones.) We have institutions for reasons, and we judge the institutions by how well they serve our reasons for having them.

This entanglement of institutional capacity with goodness entails two reasons why the enforcement of subsidiarity requires inescapably political judgments.

First, and most important, no legal authority can help judges to determine which collective ends are worth pursuing. That is an ultimate value judgment about which the Constitution is largely silent, and so is an appropriate object of democratic deliberation. Is there a more legitimate interest in economic than in noneconomic matters? Should we be troubled by endangered species, or the draining of wetlands, or the cloning of human beings? Which kinds of discrimination should be prohibited? Which kinds of association are so valuable as to be worthy of protection? The answers to these questions are not procedural. They are the stuff of substantive politics. The right to vote doesn't mean much if a little elite gets to decide which issues are allowed onto the agenda at all.[59]

Second, even if judges know what ends ought to be pursued, they have a limited ability to compare the capacities of institutions to pursue those ends. They do not have comparative data, nor have they any way to obtain such data. If they try to decide such matters, their political biases inevitably rush to fill the vacuum. This problem has led courts in Europe to be wary of deciding subsidiarity questions, despite much clearer constitutional authorization than the U.S. Supreme Court has. In the face of a clear textual mandate, the German Constitutional Court has often declined to consider whether federal legislation is "necessary," holding that "necessity" is a matter for legislative discretion.[60] Similarly in the European Union, where the principle of subsidiarity is expressly relied on by the Maastricht and Lisbon Treaties, the principle is enforced by the European Court of Justice in only the most general terms.[61] To date that court has resisted suggestions that the principle is nonjusticiable but has "showed a certain lack of enthusiasm for examining whether it had in fact been respected," leading commentators to conclude that "the Court is likely to allow the Community legislature a wide discretion in areas which involve policy choices."[62]

Chief Justice Rehnquist understood this problem. He criticized a rule that he thought "requires courts to make subjective judgments as to operational effects, for which neither their expertise nor their access to data fits them."[63] But judgment about operational effects is precisely what the principle of subsidiarity calls for.

Justice Scalia writes that subsidiarity is not a "principle of law" in the United States but only "a desideratum of policy." Even as an "aspiration rather than a legal rule," subsidiarity "deserve[s] a place alongside such other unquestionably true and indubitably unhelpful propositions as 'do good and avoid evil' and 'buy low and sell high.'"[64]

The Court might resolve the problem in the way that the European Court has: by enforcing the principle of subsidiarity only when the contested act "has been vitiated by manifest error or misuse of powers, or...the institution concerned has manifestly exceeded the limits of its discretion."[65] But this way of reading the law leaves to the legislature most of the work of looking after the principle. The Court has shown little inclination to go down that road. It has sometimes been willing to craft new constraints on federal power, unsupported by text or precedent, solely in order to maintain its own monopoly on constitutional interpretation.[66]

As noted earlier, because there is a unified national economy, courts do not and should not demand proof of collective action problems before sustaining economic regulations. With respect to noneconomic regulations, such as environmental laws, all that it makes sense for courts to ask for is (1) a plausible description of a collective action problem and (2) the failure of states to solve it.[67] This would hardly be a toothless test. Some laws conspicuously flunk it. As we have already seen, neither (1) nor (2) was available in *Lopez*.

The basic dilemma for the Court is that if it applies a deferential standard of review, then it will only invalidate unimportant, symbolic legislation like that at issue in *Lopez*, and thus it will not play any significant role in determining the balance of power between the federal government and the states. On the other hand, if it takes an aggressive role, then the constitutionality of any federal statute will depend on whether the judges regard it as a good idea that ought to have been enacted.

WHY THE MANDATE IS CONSTITUTIONAL

Under settled law at the time that the ACA was enacted, the mandate is obviously constitutional. That is why the Democrats paid so little attention to the constitutional objections. Here is the case for its constitutionality under existing precedent, in four sentences. *Insurance is commerce. Congress can regulate it. Therefore, Congress can ban discrimination on the basis of preexisting conditions. Under the Necessary and Proper Clause, it gets to decide what means it may employ to make that regulation effective.*

But we have acknowledged the flaws in settled law. So let's start over by assuming a better reading of congressional power than the Court has yet devised.

Suppose that, as we have argued, Congress should be able to act in any case in which there is a plausible case for the separate incompetence of the states to address the problem. What would this entail about the health care mandate?

The framers did not anticipate the spectacular advances of the past 200 years in our capacity to treat disease, prolong life, and ameliorate congenital illness. Many of these innovations are expensive. So with modern medicine comes a new kind of moral horror: the patient with a treatable disease who cannot afford to pay for the treatment (which is too expensive for private charity to handle).

The spillover effects are clear. Individuals with preexisting conditions are deterred from pursuing new opportunities in states where insurers are allowed to deny them coverage.

They are locked into their jobs, they are afraid to move across state lines, and that burdens the American economy as a whole. Contagious diseases also have a tendency to cross state lines.

Health insurance regulation also presents a collective action problem. The reform of the American health care system to ensure that no one would be uninsurable or bankrupted by illness was too big a task for the states to address individually. It requires more regulatory skill than most states can muster.

How can we know that collective action problems are the reasons why states have not undertaken health care reform? Could it not rather be evidence that local preferences are different in different places, and that federalism has enabled variation of a benign sort?

It is difficult to know for certain why legislation does not get enacted. But there are several pieces of information that can be the basis of reasonable inferences. One of these is that, according to a March 2012 Kaiser poll, an overwhelming majority of Americans—69%—supported guaranteed insurance for people with preexisting conditions. (Unhappily, only 51% knew that that provision is in the ACA.)[68] Yet Massachusetts alone managed to do it effectively. If states are not delivering guaranteed insurance, it is not because the electorate likes that state of affairs. Contrast the law at issue in *Lopez*: it was obvious that nothing prevented states from banning handguns near schools, because more than forty of them already had such laws.

Massachusetts is the only state that managed to expand health insurance in the way that the new federal statute does. The state embarked on that project with some unusual advantages, which suggest that other states could not easily have replicated its success. The number of uninsured persons was relatively low when the policy was adopted. Many of the uninsured were eligible for Medicaid. The percentage of the population carrying employer-sponsored coverage was unusually high. So was per capita income, creating a larger tax pool.[69] A recent study describes the comparative obstacles faced elsewhere:

> Other states will start with very different baseline benefits generally available. For example, some states have a high penetration of high-deductible plans; others are dominated by one or two insurers with a particular set of benefits; and still others have a range of insurance products with significant differences in benefit levels. Requiring comprehensive benefits similar to Massachusetts in these states would likely entail requiring many who currently have insurance to change or upgrade their plans in order to comply. Employers would have to consider upgrading plans at great expense. This could ultimately jeopardize broader support for a reform program. Conversely, setting the [minimal level of coverage] at the least common denominator plan may leave many without adequate coverage and underinsured.[70]

All these factors were substantial obstacles to replicating what Massachusetts did.

There is also adverse selection. Any state that mandates insurance for preexisting conditions risks attracting sick people and driving away healthy ones. The magnitude of this effect is uncertain, but its effect on states' incentives is plain. There is some evidence for this effect in Massachusetts. In 2008, Massachusetts discharged 1,034 Vermont patients from inpatient care, while Vermont released only 211 patients from Massachusetts. Vermont inpatients in Massachusetts had bills three times as high as Massachusetts patients in Vermont, suggesting that sick Vermonters tended to go to Massachusetts for their expensive care. And New England has one of the country's highest rates of insurance. If Utah tried to implement universal insurance, it would face a flood of sick people from Nevada and Arizona, two states with high rates of uninsurance. It is unsurprising that Hawaii, more than 2,000 miles from the nearest border state, is the only other state with near-universal health coverage.[71]

There isn't much evidence for the notion that high levels of public support are "welfare magnets" that attract the poor across state lines,[72] but fear of creating such magnets has made it hard to ameliorate poverty. A similar dynamic is likely at work here. How great is the danger, really? It is hard to say. People make residence decisions based on a wide range of factors, including the availability of benefits. In the health insurance case, the answer probably varies from one place to another, depending on the costs of moving. For example, the heavy burdens borne by Tennessee's health care system, which eventually forced cutbacks in its TennCare program for the uninsured, may be related to the fact that its most populous city, Memphis, is bordered by Mississippi and Arkansas, which offer much lower benefits.[73] TennCare insurers are also concerned that patients from other states may be establishing residency in Tennessee in order to obtain coverage for organ transplants.[74] There are no data available on this question,[75] but it is hard to believe that no one responds to incentives when failure to do so is literally suicidal.

States are reluctant to legislate because they worry that they will lose the race to the bottom. The collective action problems mean that most states cannot reform health insurance even if they all would prefer to. It is a matter in which the states are separately incompetent. Congress has the power to regulate insurance, the Court noted in 1944, because it has power "to govern affairs which the individual states, with their limited territorial jurisdiction, are not fully capable of governing."[76]

The precise uncertainty that drives the objection, that it is hard to know when a race to the bottom is happening, is part of the collective action problem. States do not know whether they will be disadvantaged in interstate competition by having welfare-promoting legislation. This deters them from enacting it. Congress does not have this problem.

This is just the kind of case in which it makes sense to give Congress the power to act.

If the Constitution were as defective as the ACA's opponents claim it is, a regime in which national problems must remain permanently unsolved, why would it deserve our allegiance? The sensible thing to do would be to try to get free of it, to try—by amendment or judicial construction—to nullify its limits so that we can live in a humanly habitable world. To continue to live with such a perverse constitution would be mindless ancestor worship.

But the opponents of reform have been unfair to the framers. The fundamental original purpose of the Constitution is to permit the American people to seize control of their own fate. The Constitution provides a structure for us to govern ourselves. That is what Congress did when, at long last, it took on the spectacularly broken American system of health care delivery.

THREE

Bad News for Mail Robbers

No one could have anticipated the constitutional limits that the ACA supposedly transgressed. Those limits did not exist while the bill was being written. They were first devised only in the fall of 2009, quite late in the legislative process. Thereafter, scholars and judges worked hard to massage and improve them, but they never succeeded in answering obvious difficulties.

THE INVENTION OF THE CONSTITUTIONAL OBJECTION

The earliest glimmerings of the action/inaction distinction appeared in a September 1993 *Wall Street Journal* piece by David Rivkin and Lee Casey.[1] (They eventually were leading attorneys in the challenge to the ACA.) When the Court allowed broad federal authority during the New Deal, "the Framers' ghosts wept." But now, as Clinton proposed his health care reforms and Republicans offered alternatives, "the plans seem to share one fundamental assumption—that every man, woman and child in the U.S. must participate in the system. The healthy must subsidize the sick; the young must subsidize the old; the not-so-old must subsidize the very young." Only after this Tough Luck Libertarian complaint did Rivkin and Casey introduce the argument that would eventually accomplish so much: "In the new health-care system, individuals will not be forced to belong because of their occupation, employment, or business activities—as in the case of Social Security. They will be dragooned into the system for no other reason than that they are people who are here."

With the demise of Clinton's reforms, the Rivkin-Casey argument was forgotten. After Obama's election, Mark Hall wrote a preliminary analysis of the constitutional issues raised by the law. He posted it on the Social Science Research Network, a website that disseminates scholarly papers, in February 2009. He concluded that the mandate easily followed from existing Commerce Clause jurisprudence. His piece is extensively footnoted, but it cites no authority to the contrary. As we have seen, as late as June 2009, Republican senator Charles Grassley thought there was "a bipartisan consensus to have individual mandates." Even Rivkin and Casey paid little attention to the mandate. Their *Wall Street Journal* op-ed that month imaginatively argued that government-dominated health care would violate the constitutional right to privacy.[2]

The first claim that the ACA mandate was unconstitutional is a short July 10, 2009, Federalist Society paper by Peter Urbanowicz and Dennis G. Smith. In their brief paper, written over a weekend, they declared that, for the law to be valid under the commerce power, "Congress would have to explain how not doing something—not buying insurance and not seeking health care services—implicated interstate commerce." But they made only a modest effort to rebut the obvious response based on text and precedent: "The decision not to engage in affirmative conduct is arguably distinguishable from cases in which Commerce Clause regulatory authority was recognized over intra-state activity." Their bottom line was that a mandate "might be susceptible to an 'as applied' challenge from individuals who (1) never access the health care system or (2) are able to pay for their health care without using insurance." This would have barred application of the statute in a few cases at most, and possibly in none at all. The hypothetical individuals are fanciful. No one who is not a multimillionaire (whose wealth is in an unsquanderable, conservatively managed trust fund) can know for certain that they will be able to pay for all their future health needs out of pocket.

On July 14, the House committees generated a unified health care bill. The next day, the bill passed the Senate Health Committee. On July 24, a Congressional Research Service memo, determinedly evenhanded, declared that the power of Congress to require the purchase of a good or service was "a novel issue." It, too, developed no substantive argument for unconstitutionality.

It's uncertain whether the constitutional case against the mandate could ever have taken off without the growing conviction on the political Right that Obama was attempting something monstrous, an unprecedented intrusion on our liberties. The intensity of that conviction became apparent during the congressional recess in August, when all over the country in a coordinated campaign, opponents screamed and booed at town hall meetings held by members of Congress. Sarah Palin began spreading the ridiculous lie that the bill would require "death panels" to decide who was worthy of medical care. (A CNN poll in September found that 41% of Americans believed her.) Representative Joe Wilson interrupted Obama's address to Congress in September by shouting "You lie!" after the president said that his bill would not cover illegal immigrants. There was a passionate desire to show that there was something fundamentally evil about the ACA. It was perhaps inevitable that this mood would eventually congeal into a constitutional objection.

An August 17 blog post by Rob Natelson offered a litany of briefly stated constitutional objections, most of which were never heard from again. It was quoted sympathetically, but without elaboration, by David Kopel on the Volokh Conspiracy, a libertarian/conservative law blog that became the most important incubator for the constitutional objections. On August 22, a *Washington Post* op-ed by Rivkin and Casey revived their claim that Congress "does not have the power to regulate Americans simply because they are there." This might mean that some people would have to go without insurance, but "advocates of universal health coverage must accept that Congress's power, like that of the other branches, has limits. These limits apply regardless of how important the issue may be."

There were some follow-up posts on Volokh Conspiracy by Jonathan Adler and Ilya Somin, both of whom reluctantly concluded that the bill was authorized by current precedent. (Both later changed their minds.)

On September 18, Randy Barnett entered the fray for the first time, with posts on Politico and Volokh. Suddenly the meme went viral. On September 21, CBS News reported, "In the last few days, a new argument has emerged in the debate over Democratic health care proposals." *The O'Reilly Factor* and Fox News had picked up on the story. An outpouring of pieces, on Volokh and elsewhere, developed the constitutional objection. But even at this point, it was a sound bite, not a legal argument.

A few dissenting voices warned that the Necessary and Proper Clause was probably all the authority that the mandate needed.

The bill passed the Senate Finance Committee on October 13, and the full House of Representatives on November 7.

Rivkin and Casey elaborated their objections in a November debate on the *Pennsylvania Law Review* website. Jack Balkin responded that their arguments relied almost entirely on pre–New Deal authority, decisions that were long since obsolete.[3]

The first sustained legal argument that tried to reconcile the argument with modern precedent was published by Barnett and two coauthors in a Heritage Foundation paper on December 9. This was no casual blog post. Barnett carefully engaged with the Court's earlier decisions recognizing broad congressional power under the Commerce Clause. Like a good lawyer, he carefully characterized them as narrow holdings that did not reach the mandate. None of those cases, he argued, required persons to enter into contracts with private parties. "If Congress can mandate this, then it can mandate anything."

Barnett's biggest innovation was to read the commerce power as subject to what he called the "class of activities" test. In commerce clause analysis, Barnett claimed, the Court first asks whether the class of regulated activities substantially affects interstate commerce; then it asks whether the petitioner has engaged in the regulated activity and so is a member of the regulated class. This is consistent with *Raich*, which Barnett argued and lost, but it calls into existence a new constitutional requirement, not announced in *Raich*. The mandate flunks this requirement, because it "*does not purport to regulate or prohibit activity of any kind, whether economic or noneconomic.*"

The mandate "purports to 'regulate' inactivity by converting the inactivity of not buying insurance into commercial activity," and thus would mean that "Congress may reach the doing of nothing at all!" To uphold the mandate, "the Supreme Court would have to concede that the Commerce Clause has no limits." This often-repeated claim faced an obvious objection: *Lopez* and *Morrison*, discussed in chapter 2, had already established limits on the commerce power, and neither relied on the action/inaction distinction. Judge Laurence Silberman later explained the problem with Barnett's claim that every previous Commerce Clause case had referred to the object of regulation as "activity": "[T]hose cases did not purport to limit Congress to reach only *existing* activities. They were merely identifying the relevant conduct in a descriptive way, because the facts of those cases did not raise the question— presented here—of whether 'inactivity' can also be regulated."[4]

Barnett's more precise claim is that Congress "may not regulate the individual's decision not to purchase a service or enter into a contract." But this rule is not a serious constraint on government power. It wasn't violated by the worst abuses of Hitler or Stalin. It allows Congress to act in every case in which the citizen has voluntarily taken some action. Most of us can't realistically avoid having jobs and buying things, and it's not much consolation to be told that I can avoid oppression if I live in the woods and eat berries. This limitation is unlikely to have any application after the ACA litigation and is patently tailored to bring about a desired result in a single case. (Had Congress known about this rule, it could have gone back the next day and enacted a law requiring anyone who ever purchases medical care to then purchase health insurance for the rest of her life.) The claim also has no relation to federalism. The line between mandating and merely encouraging economic behavior is not the line "between what is truly national and what is truly local."[5]

These flaws in the argument persisted all the way to the Supreme Court. Paul Clement, who led the litigation against the ACA, declared that he was defending a crucial element of liberty: "[F]or the most part, if you want to avoid federal regulatory power, all you can do is simply exercise your right not to engage in commerce. If the mandate is constitutional, however, then you would not have that right either."[6] This depends on two dubious premises: that citizens have an important interest in avoiding federal regulatory power, and that it is realistically feasible to avoid engaging in commerce.[7] When Clement argued that sustaining the mandate would leave no limits on Congress, Justice Breyer asked him about *Lopez*. Clement responded: "*Lopez* is a limit on the affirmative exercise of people who are already in commerce. The question is, is there any other limit to people who aren't in commerce?" In a bit of creative historical fiction, he told Breyer, a few moments earlier, that the framers weren't apprehensive about the breadth of the commerce power "because it's a power that only operated once people were already in commerce."

Barnett deserves the credit he has gotten.[8] The argument was witty, sophisticated, creative, and clever. But it had little basis in existing law, and its flaws came to light almost immediately. Most important, while the December 9 paper worked hard to distinguish the earlier Commerce Clause cases, it said nothing about the most powerful basis for Congress's authority, its broad power under the Necessary and Proper Clause. The mandate was a means for carrying out the legitimate goal of insurance regulation. The Court had declared in 1934, in a phrase that, unluckily for Barnett, it would quote with approval five months after his paper: "If it can be seen that the means adopted are really calculated to attain the end, the degree of their necessity, the extent to which they conduce to the end, the closeness of the relationship between the means adopted and the end to be attained, are matters for congressional determination alone."[9]

That was an enormous obstacle to the challenge to the ACA, and it was never adequately answered.

Barnett's paper was a work in progress. The Supreme Court brief he coauthored in February 2012 implicitly acknowledged the unfinished business of the Necessary and Proper Clause by struggling for more than thirty pages with the problem.

On the other hand, Barnett wrote for an audience that was predisposed to believe anything he said. The Republicans had united against the ACA, it was likely that they were going to lose in Congress, and so the idea that they could refight that battle in the courts was mighty attractive. If a starving man opens a can of stew with a sledgehammer, that doesn't prove that the hammer is a good can opener. It just shows that the man was desperate. The constitutional objection had been floated by others, but only Barnett had actually read the Commerce Clause case law closely and constructed a fully articulated legal argument. His was the best argument available. But that isn't saying much.

The Republicans seized on his argument with alacrity. Two weeks after his paper was published, it had become the Republican party line. On December 23, every Republican (including ten senators who had previously sponsored or cosponsored legislation containing an individual mandate) voted to support Senator John Ensign's point of order against the ACA on the ground that it exceeded Congress's commerce power.[10] One aspect of that debate is relevant to the later litigation, in which judges disagreed about whether or not the mandate was a tax. In responding to the Republican objections, several Democratic senators defended the mandate as a proper exercise of the taxing power.[11]

The bill passed the Senate on December 24. On January 19, 2010, Scott Brown surprisingly won the special Senate election in Massachusetts, depriving the Democrats of their filibuster-proof majority. For a short time, it appeared that this would kill the bill, but the Democrats eventually responded by having the House enact the Senate bill while amending it through the reconciliation process, which cannot be filibustered. That had the paradoxical effect of pushing the law to the left, since conservative Democrats such as Ben Nelson and Joseph Lieberman lost their leverage; only fifty-one votes were needed to pass the reconciliation amendment. Taxes were raised on health care industries, and wealthy Medicare beneficiaries would have to pay higher fees, and a new tax was imposed on income from financial investments.[12] The bill was signed into law in March 2010.

BARNETT'S LIBERTARIANISM

By that point, the leading intellectual force behind the challenge was the memo by Barnett, who continued, throughout the ensuing litigation, to be the leading constitutional critic of the law. Let us pause to consider the philosophical assumptions that drove his challenge. Tough Luck Libertarianism is a cultural trend that takes different forms for different adherents. If I'm going to criticize it, it is incumbent on me to address it in its strongest, most attractive, and, in this context, most influential formulation.[13] Barnett's version is unusually sophisticated, and so would be worth examining even if he had had nothing at all to do with the ACA challenge.

Barnett's 1998 book, *The Structure of Liberty*, is an ambitious effort to work out libertarian principles of law from the ground up. These are justified on grounds of rule consequentialism—the idea that rules of conduct should be selected on the basis of the goodness of their consequences. He claims that his principles of justice must be respected if we are to achieve happiness, peace, and prosperity.

The book begins with an eloquent defense of the institutions of property and contract. (Barnett is the most successful legal rhetorician since Catharine MacKinnon persuaded the courts that sexual harassment is sex discrimination.) He depends heavily on the Hayekian point that everyone's knowledge of the world is incomplete, that there needs to be some way of quickly communicating to each person the effects of his or her choices on everyone else, and that price mechanisms perform this function wonderfully. The first 160 pages are as clear a statement of a liberal ideal of the rule of law, and its relation to legal rules of property and contract, as I have read. It would be valuable for anyone beginning law school.

In the second half of the book, however, his admiration for private ordering hypertrophies into a rejection of public provision of any service at all. He wants to privatize schools, prisons, courts, streets, parks, and the police. The ultimate vision is anarchist.

The basic shift in the argument occurs when he takes up the problem of public goods—goods whose producers cannot exclude the public, and which therefore will be undersupplied by the market. The classic example is lighthouses. All ships benefit from lighthouses, whether or not they contribute to the cost of maintaining them. Individual shipowners thus have a financial incentive to "free ride" on the contributions of others. No one likes to be a sucker, so there may be no contributions, and no lighthouses—unless government finances them. Other examples of public goods are clean air and water, scientific knowledge, roads, and street lighting. Such public goods are now typically supplied by taxation and government spending.

Barnett doubts that such goods are beyond the capacity of markets to supply. He worries that even if they are, it is impossible to know, absent prices, what the socially optimal level of such goods would be. He also has a more fundamental objection: that provision of public goods by taxation uses "illicit means," because it seizes private property. Even if market failure exists, it does not mean "that the requirements of justice should be ignored or overridden."[14]

Here he suddenly and without explanation has shifted from a Hayekian mode of argument, in which property rights are justified on rule-consequentialist grounds, to a Nozickian one, in which those rights are fundamental requirements of justice that must be respected regardless of consequences. Yet he offers no reason for thinking about property in nonconsequentialist terms. (Like Hayek, he has no use for claims that markets give people what they deserve.) We saw the problem when we considered the Rawls-Nozick debate in the introduction. Property rights are socially constructed. If better consequences could be obtained, or if persons would be treated more respectfully, by defining property rights in a way that permits redistributive taxation, then the requirements of justice have not been overridden at all. They have merely been defined in a different way than Barnett has in mind.[15]

If we are going to think about property in consequentialist terms, we have to ask, consequentialist for whom? Whose happiness, peace, and prosperity are we talking about?

Nikki White contracted systemic lupus erythematosus about the time she graduated from college. She soon was too sick to go to work, with stomach pains, skin lesions, and extreme fatigue. Lupus, a chronic inflammatory disease, is treatable, but treatment requires frequent monitoring for side effects. White became so ill that she had to quit her job, and like most Americans, her job provided her health insurance. She then applied to every individual insurance plan she could find, but of course no for-profit insurance company will cover someone who has chronic lupus.

She spent the rest of her short life fighting the Medicaid bureaucracy to try to obtain coverage—coverage that of course would not exist in Barnett's ideal world, where there would be no Medicaid. Meanwhile her health steadily deteriorated. She suffered a seizure and was taken to the emergency room. Barred from releasing her until her condition was stabilized, the hospital spent about $900,000 treating complications that could have been prevented if she had been able to afford ordinary medical care. After multiple surgeries, she died at the age of thirty-two. "Nikki didn't die of lupus," her doctor told a reporter. "Nikki died from complications of the failing American health care system."[16] If she had lived in any rich country other than the United States, she would be alive today.

What has Barnett to say to the Nikki Whites of the world? The closest he comes to an answer is his uncharacteristically cursory and superficial response to Rawls. Something like Rawls's view underlies the Affordable Care Act, which goes a long way toward guaranteeing that no American citizen is ever again placed in Nikki White's position.

Barnett thinks that any conception of distributive justice faces two insuperable difficulties: first, "the task of determining who will have their resources taken away and who will be the beneficiary of the taking,"[17] which has no clear answer and thus will be the subject of factional politics; and second, the negative incentive effects on producers and costs of coercive enforcement. Any conception of distributive justice is subject to errors of application. When those errors occur, "innocent people will be jailed, their incomes attached, their homes and businesses confiscated. Lives will be ruined."[18] (Barnett supposes that those who disagree with the system of redistributive taxation will forcibly resist and therefore be punished. That is not what typically happens in the modern United States.) But of course any property rules require coercion. Barnett resists broad rights such as a right to health care, because any rights legitimate the use of violence to secure them. *"The more rights we recognize the more violence we legitimate."*[19] But what do you suppose will happen if Nikki White walks into a pharmacy and grabs a bottle of medicine that she needs in order to stay alive?

There is plenty of room for uncertainty and disagreement about what a social contract includes. But the idea of a social contract clearly rules out some social arrangements. The libertarians' hero, John Locke, thought that no one could possibly consent to a regime in which he would starve to death. Lockean property rights thus came with a proviso that everyone's basic subsistence needs would have to be provided for.[20] The same logic applies to basic medical needs. Neither Nikki White, nor anyone whose own family members might be in her position (a group that includes everyone who is not extremely rich), could possibly agree to Barnett's political principles.

Barnett thinks that because decentralization works so well for markets, it would also be good for the use of coercive force: different courts should compete for customers. (H. L. Mencken defined an idealist as "one who, on noticing that a rose smells better than a cabbage, concludes that it will also make better soup.") The ideal political order is one in which "multiple legal systems exercise the judicial function and multiple law-enforcement agencies exercise the executive function."[21] There would be no state with a monopoly of coercive force to resolve disputes between these entities. All power would be private power, regulated by contract. Barnett is remarkably confident that power in such a system would be exercised well. Individuals would each have the right to enforce their own rights of restitution, self-defense, and preventive detention. Imprisonment would be justified only when necessary to guarantee the speed and certainty of restitution, and private detention centers would employ the offenders in productive labor. If someone wrongly exercised private enforcement power against you, you could go to court and sue them for it. Evidently bad law-enforcement institutions would be subject to coercive discipline by good ones. It goes without saying that redistribution would be impossible.

Barnett thinks that the consequences would be peace and prosperity, because it is not in the interests of repeat players to seek short-term gains at the cost of long-term conflict.[22] But we don't have to go to hypothetical worlds in order to find situations in which such cooperation fails to emerge. The experiment of having multiple armed factions trying to exercise control over the same geographic area has been tried many times. The consequence, Jeffrey Winters's exhaustive survey found, is a system of warring oligarchies—prehistoric societies and medieval Europe are his principal illustrations—in which any peace is fragile and temporary. There are few modern examples. One is the mid-twentieth-century Mafia Commission in the United States. It was predicated on the value of cooperation, which promised and often delivered huge financial benefits for all participants, but its equilibrium was punctuated by frequent wars and assassinations.[23]

Libertarianism aims to shrink the domain of state power, leaving citizens to make the best deals they can with one another, given the resources they happen to have. Samuel Freeman has observed that this vision of a just society is not liberalism, but rather resembles its ancient adversary feudalism, in which parties trade their allegiance for protection by the powerful.[24] Warring oligarchy isn't good even for the ruling class, whose lives are precarious, though they do get to lord it over the serfs. But the real effect of Barnett's intervention in the contemporary United States is not likely to be anarchy, but the continuing erosion of public services and consequent reduction of the tax burden at the top, while a centralized state continues to vigorously protect private property: feudalism without the disadvantages.

The benefits of being rich in such a system would be magnified by Barnett's peculiar understanding of criminal law, which discards deterrence and retribution and would demand only that criminals make restitution. We don't need to worry, he says, that the rich would be inadequately deterred from crime: "The wealthy tend to place a very high subjective premium on their social standing and other sorts of reputational effects that would be severely damaged by a successful prosecution."[25] But the wealthy, as he concedes elsewhere,[26] is a heterogeneous and poorly defined group. "Sue me if you dare! My father is Li Gang!," said the twenty-three-year-old son of a Chinese police official after his drunken speeding killed a woman. Public pressure eventually forced authorities to criminally prosecute him. Not in Barnett's world.

Barnett's philosophy is good news if you're prosperous and healthy. It's bad news for Nikki White. Barnett's book never confronts the question of what to do about people like her. The death of Nikki White in Barnett's philosophy is like the death of Miles Archer in *The Maltese Falcon*: it is the most important issue, but the reader is cleverly kept thinking about something else. She has to accept her tough luck, because it would be unjust, a violation of people's rights, if the state were to use its coercive power of taxation to aid her. Such early, preventable deaths are not a problem at all. They show that we live in a just society.

Now, of course, in this early work, Barnett is doing pure political philosophy, not constitutional law. Why think that it has anything to do with his constitutional arguments?

There are three Randy Barnetts: the political philosopher, the constitutional theorist, and the litigator. Sometimes they say inconsistent things, for the best of reasons: Barnett the constitutional theorist understands that there are provisions in the Constitution, such as the authorization of the federal income tax, that would not exist in his ideal world, and Barnett the litigator understands that there is established precedent that departs from his reading of the Constitution. The litigator reluctantly takes as given legal rules that the other two find repellent: "Nothing about existing Supreme Court doctrine needs to change for us to prevail in this case."[27] Yet there is a crucial continuity among the three: all are centrally committed to liberty, and all understand liberty to mean the absence of government. Barnett's constitutional theory is set out in another of his books, *Restoring the Lost Constitution*. It is presented as an elaboration and defense of originalism. Yet remarkably often, it reaches conclusions that coincide with his libertarian prepossessions. Modern constitutional law, he argues, has gone wrong in two different ways: federal powers have been read too broadly—he deplores the influence of *McCulloch* and the New Deal Revolution—and the liberty-granting provisions have been read too narrowly. The Constitution, he thinks, requires a far smaller federal government than we have now, and the liberties protected by the Constitution should invalidate any state laws that are not necessary to protect individuals from harm. Steven Calabresi, a leading originalist scholar, argues that Barnett is inconsistent: the power-granting clauses are read grudgingly, to mean as little as possible, while the liberty-protective provisions are read with a breadth that would have surprised anyone at the time of the framing, for example, by invalidating restrictions of gambling, drugs, and extramarital sex.[28]

Barnett usefully distinguishes between constitutional interpretation and constitutional construction. He notes that "there is often a gap between abstract or general principles of the kind found in the Constitution and the rules of law that are needed to put those principles into action. This does not mean, however, that the choice of rules is unguided by these abstract or general principles."[29] Judges must create new rules in order to give effect to those principles. "Given the limits of interpretation, construction is inevitable and the Constitution would not long survive without it."[30] For example, the Commerce Clause rules we examined in chapter 2 are judicial constructions. The *Lopez* standards do not appear in the text of the Constitution.

Barnett's approach to construction necessarily relies on his broader understanding of the Constitution's purposes, and that understanding conveniently happens to coincide with his larger political vision. He argues that vague terms in the text—such as Congress's broad power to regulate commerce among the several states—"should be given the meaning that is most respectful of the rights of all who are affected."[31] And these rights bear an amazing resemblance to the libertarian, antigovernment rights delineated in *The Structure of Liberty*. So it is unsurprising that he concludes that the Constitution "may be the most explicitly libertarian governing document ever actually enacted into law."[32] This presumption offers an answer to Calabresi: Barnett's libertarianism does not purport to be an inference from original sources, but a permissible construction, perhaps a mandatory construction if his political theory is correct. In that case, however, it depends on the soundness of that political theory.

We've already said a bit about the evolution of Barnett's claims against the ACA. He eventually formulated that claim in terms of a liberty right: "Unless they voluntarily choose to engage in activity that is within Congress's power to regulate or prohibit, the American people retain their sovereign power to refrain from entering into contracts with private parties."[33] Or, as he put it more precisely in the Supreme Court brief he coauthored for the National Federation of Independent Business, Congress can regulate under the commerce power "only where the regulated conduct itself (1) substantially interferes with interstate commerce or its regulation, (2) is either economic in nature or an impediment to the effective execution of a commercial regulatory scheme, and (3) could be regulated without effectively authorizing plenary federal power. None of the mandate's asserted justifications satisfies these requirements."[34] Requirement 1 demands that, before someone can be regulated, they must be actively doing something, and what they are doing must in some way be interfering with commerce. Requirement 2 demands that what they are doing either be economic or be interfering with something economic.

Of these, 1 and 2 are doing all the work, since 3 can be satisfied by any limitation at all on federal power—and that limitation is already provided by *United States v. Lopez*. In fact, 3 would be satisfied by the Court's acceptance of 1 and 2, so as an element of a test for congressional power, it is redundant. Requirements 1 and 2 are potent limitations. The only trouble with them is that they would be new law: they had never been declared in any Supreme Court opinion. We are back to the question whether this makes any sense as a limitation on federal power. It does if and only if the limitation of government power is a good thing in itself. To learn Barnett's reasons for thinking that, we must go back to *The Structure of Liberty*. The three Randy Barnetts have a lot in common.

The Constitution was adopted specifically to give Congress power adequate to address the nation's problems. That is its fundamental and overriding purpose. A situation in which neither the states nor the federal government could solve the country's problems was what we had under the Articles of Confederation. It is precisely what the Constitution was intended to prevent. Yet on Barnett's reading of the Constitution, the existence of large numbers of people without adequate health care is a problem that no one can address.

Concededly, his constitutional arguments did not gut the entire ACA (absent severability arguments, which he gave little attention). He did say, repeatedly, that a single-payer plan would be constitutional. He sincerely believed that the rationales upon which the mandate was being defended would create unlimited congressional power over the economy. His argument did not block the ACA's free Medicaid for the poorest citizens, or its subsidies for those up to 400% of the poverty line. On the other hand, single-payer is politically impossible. Barnett knew that. His argument interpreted the Constitution in a way that provided no realistic possibility of insuring Nikki White, at least until she became indigent. The incapacity of any American government, state or federal, to address the problem of preexisting conditions would have become a permanent feature of the constitutional landscape. The Constitution says nothing like that, so why read it that way?

The Structure of Liberty answers the puzzle: Barnett does not believe that there *are* any common problems that a national government is necessary to solve. On the contrary, the absence of government power is *always* good for human freedom. If we don't need the state to protect us from violence, then of course we don't need it to look after our health care. The government's inability to help Nikki White is not a bug in Barnett's Constitution. It is a feature.

THE PATH TO THE SUPREME COURT

Lawsuits were filed against the law hours after it was signed, March 23, 2010. They got a remarkably sympathetic hearing from two federal district judges, Henry Hudson and Roger Vinson. In each case, courts had been chosen where congenial judges sat: Florida attorney general Bill McCollum bypassed the courthouse a few blocks from his Tallahassee office and filed in Pensacola, a district court with only three judges, all conservative Republican appointees. (Vinson was one of these.) In August, Hudson denied a motion to dismiss, and in October, so did Vinson. "Never before has the Commerce Clause and associated Necessary and Proper Clause been extended this far," Hudson wrote. It was fortunate for the challengers that Hudson was the first judge to hear the case: for years he had held stock in a Republican consulting firm whose clients had included Ken Cuccinelli, the Virginia attorney general who was plaintiff in the ACA case. In December, Hudson ruled that the mandate was unconstitutional. Vinson reached the same judgment in January 2011, but he then struck down the entire statute. His invalidation of the mandate, but not of the rest of the law, was upheld by the Eleventh Circuit Court of Appeals in August. Hudson's decision was vacated when the Fourth Circuit held that the suit was barred by the Anti-Injunction Act, which bars suits to avoid the payment of taxes.[35] Three other district judges—in Michigan, the Western District of Virginia, and the District of Columbia—summarily threw out the challenges.[36] The Sixth and D.C. Circuits both held that the mandate was constitutional. Notably, two Republican-appointed court of appeals judges of unimpeachable conservative credentials, Lawrence Silberman and Jeffrey Sutton, both could find no constitutional objection to the mandate.

A few states cited federalism concerns to justify laws that sought to nullify the ACA, declaring that their citizens did not need to comply with the mandate. These are obviously void under the clause proclaiming the Constitution and federal law the "supreme Law of the Land," and they received little attention. The more serious challenge, and the one that we shall now focus on, is that the mandate is unconstitutional.

Hudson and Vinson wrote the most important lower court opinions, because they gave plausibility to what until that point had been dismissed as frivolous arguments. The constitutional objections to the bill had already been given credibility by their frequent repetition during the December 2009 debates. Now they had the imprimatur of two federal judges, in widely publicized decisions. (The courts that upheld it—and there were more of them—got less prominent news coverage.)[37] Because these decisions transformed the debate, lending the objections judicial approval, it is worth examining their reasoning in some detail.

Hudson and Vinson had to contend with both the commerce power and the Necessary and Proper Clause, which, we have seen, provided ample federal authority for the mandate. How did they address these difficulties?

Begin with the commerce power. Both judges declared that the action/inaction distinction was a limit upon its exercise. Hudson wrote that in order to be subject to regulation by Congress, an individual had to engage in "some type of self-initiated action." Vinson similarly argued that failure to purchase health insurance is "inactivity,"[38] and Congress cannot regulate inactivity.

Vinson acknowledged that there was no authority for the activity/inactivity distinction but quoted *Lopez* for the proposition that, unless the commerce power is somehow limited, it would be "difficult to perceive any limitation on federal power." If Congress can regulate inactivity, it "could do almost anything it wanted," and "we would have a Constitution in name only." We have already seen the difficulty with this argument: *Lopez* constrains congressional power without relying on the activity/inactivity distinction. The authority on which Vinson relies undermines the point he is trying to make.

The two judges' effort to navigate around the Necessary and Proper Clause is painful to watch. Both supposed that the commerce power is somehow a limit on Congress's power to choose appropriate means. "If a person's decision not to purchase health insurance at a particular time does not constitute the type of economic activity subject to regulation under the Commerce Clause," Hudson declared, "then logically, an attempt to enforce such provision under the Necessary and Proper Clause is equally offensive to the Constitution."[39] By the same "logic," if I cannot pick up a pencil with my brain, then it follows that I cannot do it with my hand either. This reads the Necessary and Proper Clause out of the Constitution completely, and inverts the *McCulloch* principle. Try this reasoning in a few other constitutional contexts. If locking up mail robbers is no part of the operation of a post office, then an attempt to do that under the Necessary and Proper Clause is equally offensive to the Constitution. If growing marijuana for one's own consumption is not regulable economic activity, then it too is immune from federal law.

Vinson acknowledged, and even quoted, Chief Justice Marshall's declaration in *McCulloch* that if "the end be legitimate," then "all means which are appropriate, which are plainly adapted to that end...are constitutional." And then he admitted that, under the settled meaning of the commerce power, which he did not question,[40] "regulating the health care insurance industry (including preventing insurers from excluding or charging higher rates to people with pre-existing conditions)" is a legitimate end. But, *three sentences later*, he declared: "The Necessary and Proper Clause cannot be utilized to 'pass laws for the accomplishment of objects' that are not within Congress's enumerated powers." Did he so quickly forget that he had just admitted that the object *was* within Congress's enumerated powers?

Vinson noted that the government has "asserted again and again that the individual mandate is absolutely 'necessary' and 'essential' for the Act to operate as it was intended by Congress. I accept that it is." Indeed, because the mandate was so necessary to the legislative scheme, he declared it nonseverable and invalidated the entire law.[41] Recall that *McCulloch* rejected Maryland's claim that the Necessary and Proper Clause only authorized laws that were absolutely necessary to the exercise of an enumerated power. Any means that was "convenient," *McCulloch* held, was within Congress's discretion. But Vinson's stipulated necessity implies that *even if* McCulloch *had come out the other way*—even if Marshall had accepted Maryland's claim that any congressional action must be *absolutely* necessary to the exercise of an enumerated power—the mandate would still not be authorized by the Necessary and Proper Clause.

Vinson did suggest a more definite limitation on congressional power: the Necessary and Proper Clause cannot be invoked if the problem Congress is trying to address is Congress's own fault. Here is the argument:

> [R]ather than being used to implement or facilitate enforcement of the Act's insurance industry reforms, the individual mandate is actually being used as the means to avoid the adverse consequences of the Act itself. Such an application of the Necessary and Proper Clause would have the perverse effect of enabling Congress to pass ill-conceived, or economically disruptive statutes, secure in the knowledge that the more dysfunctional the results of the statute are, the more essential or "necessary" the statutory fix would be. Under such a rationale, the more harm the statute does, the more power Congress could assume for itself under the Necessary and Proper Clause. This result would, of course, expand the Necessary and Proper Clause far beyond its original meaning.

If, however, Congress has no power to address negative consequences that follow from its own statutory scheme, then Marshall was wrong about mail robbery after all. Mail robbery is an adverse consequence of Congress's decision to establish a post office: had it not done that, all those valuable documents would not be gathered together in one place. But, you might say, *That is crazy; of course Congress can decide that it's worth having a post office, even if establishing one creates negative side effects, which then must be addressed.* If, as Vinson admitted, Congress can also decide that people with preexisting conditions can be protected, then these cases are indistinguishable.

Barnett saw the problem. His solution was to note that the New Deal Court had never expressly abandoned the narrow definition of commerce as trade. Instead, it allowed broad congressional power under the Necessary and Proper Clause. The question, then, was not the reach of commerce but power under the Necessary and Proper Clause. Here, however, he had to contend with the deferential reading of that clause. His solution, which went to press as Vinson issued his opinion, was to reason by analogy with earlier cases that had said that Congress could not commandeer state governments to carry out its programs. By the same logic, he argued, it could not commandeer individuals, either.[42] The analogy distorted the anticommandeering cases, which turned on the idea that Congress had "the power to regulate individuals, not States."[43]

On appeal, the Eleventh Circuit Court of Appeals affirmed Vinson's decision holding the mandate unconstitutional, but reversed his decision to strike down the entire act. In response to the Necessary and Proper Clause argument, which Vinson had handled so badly, the appeals court in effect declares that it is none of Congress's business if people go without insurance and transfer their health care costs to others: "An individual's uninsured status in no way interferes with Congress's ability to regulate insurance companies." This presumes that Congress is indifferent to the consequences of its regulatory scheme: it just likes to regulate insurance companies. Congress's declared aim in the statute, how-ever, is to reduce the number of the uninsured. The opinion goes on: "At best, the individual mandate is designed *not* to enable the execution of the Act's regulations, but to counteract the significant regulatory costs on insurance companies and adverse consequences stemming from the fully executed reforms. That may be a relevant political consideration, but…" So now the frustration of the stat-ute's declared purpose is merely a "political consideration."

A final problem for these federal courts was the fact that the mandate functions as a tax. It is a provision in the Internal Revenue Code that deducts a monetary sum from the tax refund of a per-son who goes without health insurance. Even if you somehow suppose that the mandate exceeds the commerce power, it would be valid anyway as an exercise of the power to tax. Congress has a general power to "collect Taxes" to provide for the "general Welfare of the United States." The taxing power is not limited to objects of interstate commerce. A tax, the Court held in 1950, does not become unconstitutional "because it touches on activi-ties which Congress might not otherwise regulate."[44]

Hudson and Vinson, and many after them, declared that the mandate is not a tax because some of the law's sponsors sometimes claimed that it was not, and because the statute declared that it was based on the commerce power. They were certainly right about the statute's evasiveness. Contemporary American politics has become a ritual of dueling mendacities, in which Republicans claim that taxes can be slashed with no reduction in public services and Democrats claim that those services can be enhanced with no increase in taxes; this statute was an example. But the two judges' reasoning would create two previously unheard-of doctrines: that federal courts have authority to police the public statements of politicians, and that Congress must expressly invoke all possi-ble constitutional bases for legislation.[45] A leading defense of this proposed rule is Paul Clement's Supreme Court brief: "[A]ny conception that the structural provisions of the Constitution ensure accountability in government decision-making is surely offended by the notion that Congress can enact legislation that would not have passed had it been labeled a tax and then turn around and defend it as a valid exercise of the tax power."[46] Clement hypothesizes a peculiar lot of voters, who are mesmerized by labels, and don't even always pay attention to those. The version of the ACA that passed in the House was clearly labeled a tax. In the final debate in the Senate, several senators expressly invoked the taxing power in support of the law. The voters that Clement imagines are also oblivious to counterspeech by opponents of a pending law: Republicans continually insisted that the mandate was a tax. If voters are this dumb, then accountability is a lost cause.

Vinson also repeatedly suggested that whenever Congress does something it has not done before, its action is presumptively unconstitutional. These new rules would, if consistently applied, randomly blow up large parts of the U.S. Code. This is constitutional interpretation undertaken in the spirit of a saboteur in wartime.

THE BROCCOLI HORRIBLE

These arguments were feeble, but they were powerfully undergirded by what Judge Ginsburg called the Broccoli Horrible.[47] (She was referring to a form of argument familiar to lawyers, the "parade of horribles" that allegedly will follow if one's opponent's argument is accepted.) Judge Vinson worried that "Congress could require that people buy and consume broccoli at regular intervals."[48] Broccoli became the central trope of the health care debate. It was mentioned eight times in the Supreme Court arguments, and twelve times in the opinions. A Google search of "health care reform" + broccoli in August 2012 produced 226,000 hits. I discuss it separately from the doctrinal arguments, because it is mysterious just what kind of constitutional argument it is supposed to be. Is it about the Commerce Clause? The Necessary and Proper Clause? It's not clear. It is a kind of freestanding rhetorical gesture.

The Broccoli Horrible rests on several mistakes. One of these is mushing two claims together, so that the weaker one sneakily borrows support from the stronger, but less relevant, one. Almost certainly, government can't make you *eat* broccoli. That would likely violate the constitutional right to bodily integrity that supports, for example, the right to refuse unwanted medical treatment.[49] (As I'll explain shortly, no court will ever decide the issue because no such law could ever get passed.) But there is no such right to economic liberty. The economic claim collapses once it is decoupled from the bodily integrity claim. If, under *Morrison*, Congress has plenary authority over the economy, then it *can* make you *buy* broccoli.

How scary is that? It's hard to see how such a law could be justified. It would be an abuse of Congress's broad authority under *Morrison*, because the law would not be addressing any collective action problem. But this hypothetical isn't an objection to the mandate that Congress actually enacted. There are manifest differences between broccoli and health insurance: no one unavoidably needs broccoli, it is not unpredictable when one will need broccoli, broccoli is not expensive, providers are permitted by law to refuse it, and there is no significant cost-shifting in the way it is provided.

Here we come to the Broccoli Horrible's second mistake: treating a slippery slope argument as a logical one, when in fact it is an empirical one. Any slippery slope argument depends on a prediction that doing the right thing in the instant case will, in fact, increase the likelihood that future decision makers, whose judgment is less reliable than ours, will do the wrong thing in the danger case.[50] If there is no danger, then the fact that there logically could be has no weight.

Government has lots of scary powers that the judiciary can't protect us from. It can declare stupid wars. It can ruin the economy through mismanagement. The federal taxing power empowers the government to tax incomes at 100%. Relax! It won't happen. When Professor John Hart Ely argued in 1980 that the courts should not create unenumerated rights, he elicited the objection that there would then be no protection from dumb and oppressive laws, such as a ban on the removal of diseased gall bladders. He responded: "[I]t can only deform our constitutional jurisprudence to tailor it to laws that couldn't be enacted, since constitutional law appropriately exists for those situations where representative government cannot be trusted, not for those where we know it can."[51] Paul Clement's brief declares: "The only explanation for the utter absence of comparable mandates is the utter absence of constitutional authority to enact them."[52] Democracy, however, sometimes explains why legislatures don't do things they have the power to do.

The slippery slope we should be focusing on is the one on the other side, the danger that judicial fears of centralizing power lead the courts to incapacitate the United States from addressing real, pressing problems. That, we saw in chapter 2, is a danger that has repeatedly become real.

Similarly with the Broccoli Horrible. The fear rests on one real problem: there are lots of private producers, including many in agriculture, who will lobby to use the coercive power of the federal government to transfer funds from your pockets into theirs. The last thing they want to do, however, is impose duties on individuals, because then the individuals will know that they have been burdened. There are too many other ways to get special favors in a less visible way. So Congress is never going to try to make you eat your broccoli.[53]

On the other hand, you are probably already consuming more high-fructose corn syrup than is good for you. Subsidies for the production of corn have produced huge surpluses of the syrup, which in turn becomes a cheap ingredient of mass-produced food and turns up in lots of stuff you eat. So consumers have to face obesity, diabetes, and rotten teeth, but no mandate! You and I are paying for this travesty, and it is happening in such a low-visibility way that many of us never realize that Dracula has been paying regular visits. The Broccoli Horrible thus distracts attention from the real problem, one that will not be addressed by the action/inaction distinction (and that isn't curable by any rule of constitutional law).

Perhaps the most potent source of the Broccoli Horrible's power is its resonance with conservative fears, tinged with gender anxiety, about the welfare state. Jared Goldstein observes that it "calls to mind an overbearing mother who thinks she knows what's best for us and can tell us what to do," and thus evokes a "nanny state" in which "Mommy is in power."[54] The fear of being thus infantilized and emasculated elicits an instinctive revulsion.

As against the nanny state, opponents of the ACA propose a vision that I'll call "I Am a Rock." It claims that if I'm not actively engaged in interstate commerce, I'm somehow immune from federal regulation. Justice Kennedy, at oral argument, was troubled that the mandate "requires the individual to do an affirmative act." Tough Luck Libertarianism rests on a vision of the heroic solitary individual, who sustains himself without any external support.

Ayn Rand is the most widely read delineator of this kind of hero. Without her enormous cultural influence, it is uncertain whether Tough Luck Libertarianism could have gotten enough political traction to help sustain the health care challenge. When she told the story of how she came to the United States as a penniless Russian immigrant, she declared: "No one helped me, nor did I think at any time that it was anyone's duty to help me."[55] Actually, she spent her first months here fed and housed by relatives in Chicago, who also helped her with loans of cash. She never paid them back, even when she became rich.[56] Her vision rests on the denial of one's own dependence and vulnerability. A kind of psychic splitting appears to be going on, in which the weak and helpless aspects of the self are projected onto a despised other. Rand's contemporary popularity is curious. She was never as politically influential as she wished to be, in large part because American conservatism was Christian, and Rand despised Christianity. Today's conservatism is no less overtly Christian, but somehow Christianity manages to coexist happily with Tough Luck Libertarianism.

Paul Simon's lyric was intentionally ironic, because he knew that Donne was right: no man is an island. The notion that there is some corner where I can go and hide with my money, free from any obligations to anyone else, ignores the fact that the political and economic structure is what made it possible for me to have that money. I didn't have my Charles Schwab brokerage account in the state of nature. This vision is also in denial about the fact that no one is self-sufficient: sooner or later I will be old and sick and in need of care.

The Florida attorney general argued for a substantive constitutional right "to make personal healthcare decisions without governmental interference."[57] Near the end of his opinion, in a dictum that evidently reveals what is really bothering him, Hudson writes: "At its core, this dispute is not simply about regulating the business of insurance—or crafting a system of universal health insurance coverage—it's about an individual's right to choose to participate."

The opinions of Roberts and the Scalia group have their extravagances, which we'll consider shortly, but they steered clear of this kind of claim. The Supreme Court rejected the purported "inherent right of every freeman to care for his own body and health in such way as to him seems best" in 1905, in *Jacobson v. Massachusetts.*[58] The claimant there asserted that mandatory smallpox vaccination violated his rights. It is true that vaccination is an imposition on one's liberty. Dying of smallpox is also an imposition on one's liberty.

Jacobson was decided the same year as *Lochner v. New York*, the Supreme Court decision striking down a maximum-hours law, which I discussed in chapter 2. Many in the legal community have regarded the constitutional objection to the mandate as a return to *Lochner*, but the "right" that the mandate is supposed to violate was too much even for the *Lochner* Court. Was *Jacobson* wrong? Does the Constitution protect the smallpox virus?

This wrinkle on Tough Luck Libertarianism is pervasive in the arguments against the law, but it is intellectually incoherent, because the argument purports to apply only against the federal government, not the states.[59] It has not been explained where this individual right is supposed to come from—it happens not to be mentioned in the text of the Constitution—or why it does not also invalidate anything that the states might do to force people into insurance pools.

FROM COURT TO COURT

There are three levels of federal courts in the United States: the district courts, the courts of appeals, and the Supreme Court. Once the Eleventh Circuit had invalidated the mandate—and especially because other circuits reached an opposite result, creating inconsistent law on a major federal issue—the case was certain to end up in the Supreme Court.

The Court scheduled an unusual six hours of oral argument. A number of complex issues justified such unprecedented length. If the Anti-Injunction Act applied, as the Fourth Circuit had held, then the case had to be dismissed and nothing could be decided about the merits. There was the mandate, of course. There was the question whether, if the mandate was invalidated, any other part of the law, or even all of it, had to be struck down as well. Finally, a sleeper issue, which had gotten little attention, was the claim that the Medicaid expansion unconstitutionally coerced the states. The Court did not need to address this argument, which the lower courts had unanimously rejected. It was too much even for Judge Vinson, who was ready to invalidate the entire act on other grounds.

The challengers' Supreme Court attorney was superlawyer Paul Clement, the former solicitor general of the United States, who had argued forty-nine cases before the Court, and taught at Georgetown and New York University. One would expect his case against the mandate to be the most powerful that anyone could make.

Yet his brief never squarely addressed the problem of the Necessary and Proper Clause. It argues that the mandate "is a law for carrying into execution a power that Congress does not have: the power to compel individuals to enter into commerce." The mandate "is exercised not to effectuate regulation of interstate commerce, but rather to *create* commerce so that Congress may regulate it."[60] This confuses ends with means. The *purpose* of the health reform law is not to compel anyone to do anything, but to guarantee that those who have been sick in the past have access to health care. The mandate is a means—it has become clear by now, an unpopular means—for accomplishing that end. Congress only used it because it had to.

If you use this trick of confusing means with end, you can invalidate any federal program you like (or, more precisely, that you don't like). Return to Chief Justice Marshall's mail robbers example in *McCulloch*. A law criminalizing mail robbery, Clement can say, is a law for carrying into execution a power that Congress does not have: the power to lock people up for mail robbery. It is exercised not to effectuate the operation of a post office but rather to imprison robbers, which is not part of mail delivery. If you run ends and means together in this way, you read the Necessary and Proper Clause out of the Constitution and invalidate quite a lot of what the federal government now routinely does. For example, it is not clear how the Environmental Protection Agency could survive, since there is no enumerated power to keep the country's air breathable or its water drinkable.

The brief argues that Congress cannot bring commerce into existence: "It could hardly be otherwise, as that limitation is essential to prevent the Commerce Clause from becoming a grant of the very police power that all concede the Constitution withholds from Congress and reserves to the States."[61] But the brief also has so many citations to *Lopez*, the 1995 case that invalidated a federal law banning possession of handguns near schools, that its table of authorities doesn't try to enumerate them. (Instead of page numbers, the table simply says "passim.") *Lopez* itself, however, imposed limits on federal power, even though the law it struck down did not try to call commerce into existence.

"There is no question that the individual mandate usurps the States' police power to protect the health and liberty of their residents."[62] Here it appears that the federal power to regulate health insurance is called into question after all. Health care

is a matter reserved to the states. Suddenly there are constitutional difficulties not only with Obama's law but with Medicare,
Medicaid, and hundreds of other federal laws.

Even after the Court granted review, it was far from clear that
the law was in trouble. For more than a year, Intrade, the prediction market website, offered a contract on whether the Court
would invalidate the mandate. The market estimated the odds at
less than 50% for most of that time, but after the oral argument in
March 2012, the odds surged, rising to nearly 80% just before the
Court ruled. The judges' unexpectedly withering questioning
of Solicitor General Donald Verrilli at the oral argument, and
their gentleness to Clement, changed everything. Studies have
found that, at Supreme Court oral argument, the lawyer who is
asked more questions is more likely to lose.[63] Verrilli was asked
more than 100 questions, his opponents only 87; Roberts interrupted Verrilli 23 times, his opponents 7. No wonder Verrilli
looked bad. He was given a much harder time than Clement, by
judges already inclined to rule against him. And it would have
been hard to anticipate the kind of questions he got, examples of
which were cited in the introduction.

I was the correspondent who covered the argument for
Salon.com, an online magazine. After intensively studying the
oral arguments, and particularly the recurring Tough Luck
Libertarian arguments, all day for three days, my feeling at the
end was relief that I would not have to spend any more time in
the company of these people.

After the oral argument, Obama was uncharacteristically
inarticulate. "I am confident that the Supreme Court will not
take what would be an unprecedented, extraordinary step of
overturning a law that was passed by a strong majority of a
democratically elected Congress," he told a news conference.
This way of putting it implied that judicial review itself was

unprecedented. Obama, a former constitutional law professor, should have been able to do better than this.

Obama's clumsiness was shortly eclipsed by a crude political stunt by an all-Republican-appointed panel of the Fifth Circuit that was hearing another ACA challenge. One of the judges, with the support of the entire panel, cited Obama's statements and ordered Attorney General Eric Holder to produce a letter explaining the president's views on judicial review. It is remarkable for a court thus to respond to an out-of-court statement unrelated to the litigation before it. Holder delivered a memo lecturing the panel about the presumption that statutes are constitutional, and dryly added that the question he was answering "does not concern any argument made in the government's brief or at oral argument in this case." What the Supreme Court needed above all was the public's perception that the judiciary was above politics. This didn't help.

The political stakes were underlined by Mitt Romney shortly before the Court's decision, when he declared that, if the ACA was invalidated, "then the first three and a half years of the Obama administration will have been entirely wasted, because that's where he devoted his energy and passion."[64]

FOUR

What the Court Did

The Supreme Court's decision could easily have precipitated a humanitarian catastrophe—30 million people deprived of their health insurance, chaos as the Supreme Court smashed a statutory scheme that had already become integrated with a fifth of the American economy, all on the basis of terrible legal arguments. Terrible arguments did carry the day, but the damage was relatively minimal. So I'm just left to fret, in typical law professor fashion, about a poorly reasoned Supreme Court decision that is going to confuse courts in future cases. Its most consequential move was its modification of Medicaid, and even that, in the end, may not have much effect.

The Court split, 4–1–4, with Roberts in the middle. Justices Ginsburg and Sotomayor wanted to uphold the whole thing. Justices Scalia, Kennedy, Thomas, and Alito wanted to strike it all down. (Thomas wrote a brief separate dissent reiterating his desire to demolish modern Commerce Clause doctrine.) Justices

Breyer and Kagan agreed with Roberts that the Medicaid condition was unconstitutional. Because Roberts had at least five votes for whatever he wanted to do, his views prevailed on every issue, even when no other justice joined his reasoning.

He began by addressing the Tax Anti-Injunction Act, which says that a tax cannot be challenged in court until it has been paid, and which the Fourth Circuit had decided barred the suit. If it applied, the act would have shut down the litigation for years, since no penalties will be collected until 2015. Roberts concluded that Congress had not intended the payment to be treated as a "tax" under the Anti-Injunction Act—which did not prevent him from saying later that it was authorized by the tax power. This produced a lot of confusion—how can it be a tax for one purpose but not the other?—but Roberts was on firm ground here. Congress gets to decide what the act applies to; it does not get to decide the constitutional question of the scope of its taxing power. Roberts here may also have been influenced by a powerful and legitimate prudential consideration: if the issue was left hanging for years, then during that time a very large sector of the American economy would not know what law was going to apply to it. The judiciary should try to avoid sowing confusion about the law.

Roberts then turned to the merits of the challenge and began by endorsing the view that the mandate was beyond the commerce power. (At this point during his reading of the opinion, CNN and Fox News prematurely announced that the Court had struck down the law.) But he then upheld the mandate as a tax, because it is only enforced by a monetary penalty withheld from tax refunds. The bottom line: the mandate is upheld. The Court struck down a provision that, if states did not comply with a massive expansion of Medicaid coverage, they could lose all their Medicaid funds.

This, Roberts held, unconstitutionally forced the states into the expanded program.

Let us consider each step of his reasoning.

THE MANDATE

The mandate, he says, is beyond Congress's powers under the commerce power, because Congress may not regulate inactivity and, specifically, may not "compel individuals not engaged in commerce to purchase an unwanted product." He thus introduces into constitutional law the action/inaction distinction. His argument is in part textual; the power to "regulate" commerce presupposes that commerce is already in existence. But he admits that there is some evidence that, at the time of the framing, "regulate" sometimes meant to direct or to command. His more basic argument is based on the structure and purposes of the Constitution. Without the action/inaction distinction, he argues, Congress would have boundless power:

> Allowing Congress to justify federal regulation by pointing to the effect of inaction on commerce would bring countless decisions an individual could *potentially* make within the scope of federal regulation, and—under the Government's theory—empower Congress to make those decisions for him.

The mandate exceeds the commerce power, Roberts argues, because it targets "a class whose commercial inactivity rather than activity is its defining feature." Tough Luck Libertarianism makes an appearance here: those affected are primarily "healthy, often young adults who are less likely to need significant health care and have other priorities for spending their money."

One charitable reading of Roberts's reasoning is that he is trying to contain the broad federal power laid down in *Gonzales v. Raich*, the medical marijuana case, and that the action/inaction distinction seems to him to be the only hope of doing that. Recall that a principal basis for the challenge to the mandate was *Raich*'s declaration that Congress may "regulate purely local activities that are part of an economic 'class of activities' that have a substantial effect on interstate commerce." As a court of appeals judge before his Supreme Court appointment, Roberts had endorsed the idea that only economic activity could be regulated under the commerce power.[1] The challengers to the statute argued that the action/inaction distinction was the only constraint left standing after this decision. If inaction can be part of a class of activities, then nothing is beyond the commerce power. The United States throughout the litigation rejected the action/inaction distinction but claimed that even if activity is a constitutional requirement, it is satisfied here. The ACA itself declared that the minimum coverage provision "regulates activity that is commercial and economic in nature: economic and financial decisions about how and when health care is paid for, and when health insurance is purchased."[2] In the Fourth Circuit, it argued that the provision "addresses the consumption of health care services without payment, which is indisputably activity."[3] In the Eleventh Circuit, it said: "People without insurance are not 'inactive'; they actively participate in the market for health care services."[4] Its Supreme Court brief described the pertinent conduct somewhat differently, as "the practice of going without health insurance and seeking to pay for health care in other ways."[5] For this reason, "the uninsured as a class are active in the market for health care, which they regularly seek and obtain."[6] If one concedes the action/inaction distinction even arguendo, then none of these formulations is convincing. "Economic and financial decisions" include decisions not to act. Those who self-insure are neither consuming services without payment nor active in the market for health care, though these things will certainly be true at some unknown time in the future. Going without health insurance is, once more, inaction. Roberts responded that "most of those regulated by the individual mandate are not currently engaged in any commercial activity involving health care."

But the real question is whether the action/inaction distinction makes any sense in this context. Roberts wrote that "the distinction between doing something and doing nothing would not have been lost on the Framers, who were 'practical statesmen,' not metaphysical philosophers." But here he has lost sight of the most basic point of the enterprise of constructing limits on congressional power. Roberts emphasizes practical statesmanship, but the action/inaction distinction is a formal, not a practical, one. The point of judicially enforced federalism is to prevent the federal government from taking over governmental tasks that can be better handled by the states. It is not to draw a line just for the sake of drawing a line. And it emphatically is not to create a state of affairs in which some problems can't be solved by any governmental entity, state or federal.

A better way of working within the terms of the action/inaction distinction, one that the government curiously never pursued in its briefs, is to observe that those regulated by the mandate are not in fact outside of commerce. The penalty is a tax on income, and you cannot generate income without engaging in commerce. This argument was made, in response to a question at oral argument in the Eleventh Circuit, by Acting Solicitor General Neal Katyal (who obviously thought that the whole exercise, and the action/inaction distinction that demanded it, was silly). It never appeared in the United States' briefs even after that.

Roberts seems to see this problem, because he later writes that "most of those regulated by the individual mandate are not currently engaged in any commercial activity *involving health care*" (emphasis added). It is not enough to be engaged in commerce; persons in one market cannot be forced to buy in another market. But federal law routinely violates this principle. Publicly traded corporations, for example, are required to hire independent auditors even though they are not in the audit market. Hazardous workplaces must have safety equipment even though they are not in the safety equipment market.[7] An unchallenged provision of the ACA requires employers not in the health care market to buy insurance for their employees. There's lots of room to manipulate the description of the relevant market, too. When the Civil Rights Act was passed in 1964, discriminatory hotels were not currently engaged in any commercial activity involving black hotel guests.

The government also paid remarkably little attention to the question of what the limits of congressional power ought to be.[8] Distinguishing *Lopez* and *Morrison*, it declared that noneconomic conduct was at issue in those cases, and that Congress may not invade traditional state matters such as family law, criminal law, or education. But this discussion was brief. Most of the case it made in the Supreme Court focuses on the unique nature of the health care market, which justified mandates in a way that it would not with, say, broccoli. The strategy is clear: asking the Court to sustain only this statute is less demanding than proposing a more general theory of the commerce power, and offers a path to a more narrow ruling. But line-drawing was the central focus of the case, and in retrospect it is clear that the United States should have given that issue more attention. The problem became painfully clear when Justice Alito asked Verrilli, "[C]ould you express your limiting principle as succinctly as you possibly can?" The heart of Verrilli's long answer was this:

> Congress can regulate the method of payment by imposing an insurance requirement in advance of the time in which the—the service is consumed when the class to which that requirement applies either is or virtually most certain to be in that market when the timing of one's entry into that market and what you will need when you enter that market is uncertain and when—when you will get the care in that market, whether you can afford to pay for it or not and shift costs to other market participants.

The flurry of subordinate clauses certainly narrows the scope of the holding that he is asking of the Court, but succinct it ain't. Roberts, after endorsing the action/inaction distinction, noted that the government had argued "that the individual mandate can be sustained as a sort of exception to this rule" because of its unique character, but he was unpersuaded of its uniqueness.

This is not, however, to defend what Roberts did. He certainly was aware of the idea that Congress should be able to legislate when the states can't. Several amicus briefs capably pressed that view.

What about the Necessary and Proper Clause? As we have seen, the challenge to the health care law always had to reckon with the broad powers of Congress under *McCulloch*. Roberts, accepting the analogy with the state-commandeering cases developed by Barnett, argues that a law, even if it is necessary, is not "proper" if permitting it would "undermine the structure of government established by the Constitution." Roberts quoted a declaration in *McCulloch* that the Necessary and Proper Clause did not authorize the use of any "'great substantive and independent power' of the sort at issue here."

Here he relies, without acknowledgment, on an attack on the mandate developed by Gary Lawson and David Kopel,[9] who argued, on the basis of a new interpretation of the historical evidence, that the clause incorporates norms from eighteenth-century agency law, administrative law, and corporate law, and that the mandate (and perhaps much else in the U.S. Code, though they are coy about this) violates those norms. The Necessary and Proper Clause, as Lawson and Kopel understand it, tightly limits the scope of implied powers to those that are less important—less "worthy" or "dignified"—than the principal powers to which they are subsidiary.

Of all the scholars who attacked the mandate, Lawson and Kopel offered the most sophisticated response to the problem presented by the Necessary and Proper Clause. Their claims, however, are obscure even on their own terms. It is mysterious how we are to know whether the power to impose a penalty for going without health insurance is less "worthy" than the power to regulate interstate commerce. The same difficulty is presented by Roberts's revival of the distinction—made in *McCulloch*, but ignored for nearly two centuries thereafter—between a "great substantive and independent power" and lesser powers. (That distinction is only mentioned in two nineteenth-century Supreme Court cases between *McCulloch* and the ACA, both upholding congressional power.) How does one know whether a power meets this description?

What is not uncertain is that the federal government now exercises unenumerated powers that are not obviously lesser to the enumerated ones. Congress's plenary authority to regulate immigration and exclude aliens sure looks like "great substantive and independent power," not merely derivative from the enumerated power "to establish a uniform Rule of Naturalization." The commerce power does not necessarily entail the power to regulate air and water pollution, or the sale of securities or adulterated food, neither of which typically is conducted across state lines.

Roberts assumes without argument that the mandate is some enormous new power. Justice Ginsburg pointed out that there have been mandates in the U.S. Code since the founding, to purchase firearms in anticipation of service in the militia, register for the draft, file a tax return, report for jury duty, and exchange gold coin for paper currency. (She didn't mention the 1798 requirement that sailors have health insurance.) Roberts responded that all of these "are based on constitutional provisions other than the Commerce Clause." But how can something be a great substantive and independent power in relation to one provision but not another? Roberts might respond that some powers inherently imply the capacity to impose mandates: the requirement of jury service has from time immemorial been part of the operation of courts, for example. But this won't work for all the mandates in question. The requirement, under the Emergency Banking Relief Act of 1933, that all persons "pay and deliver to the Treasurer of the United States any or all gold coin, gold bullion, and gold certificates" owned by them, and accept paper money in exchange, cannot be inferred from the power to coin money.

Roberts also argued that an argument authorizing the mandate "vests Congress with the extraordinary ability to create the necessary predicate to the exercise of an enumerated power." If this is permitted, "Congress could reach beyond the natural limit of its authority and draw within its regulatory scope those who otherwise would be outside of it." We have seen this argument before: it is the claim that Congress cannot arrogate to itself the power to solve problems that are of its own making. We have also seen what is wrong with it. Mail robbers are not ordinarily within the scope of the operation of a post office. Roberts thought that a new expansion of the "proper" limitation was necessary, because permitting Congress to choose these means would permit it "to reach beyond the natural extent of its authority, 'everywhere extending the sphere of its activity and drawing all power into its impetuous vortex.'" The argument here is remarkably crude: (1) There must be some limit on federal power; (2) I can't think of another one; and therefore, (3) the limit must preclude the individual mandate.

Recall the *Comstock* case, discussed in chapter two. Congress's ability to operate federal prisons—a power that, for the most part, is itself derived from the Necessary and Proper Clause—would not be impaired by the release of dangerous, mentally ill sex offenders into the general population. The *Comstock* Court nonetheless held that Congress had the power to keep such persons detained. It noted that some of those offenders "would likely *not* be detained by the States if released from federal custody, in part because the Federal Government itself severed their claim to 'legal residence in any State' by incarcerating them in remote federal prisons."[10] But that is only to say that the statutory scheme generates negative consequences, and that Congress has the power to address those consequences.

Comstock also presses hard on the "great substantive and independent power" principle. Roberts tries to distinguish *Comstock*, because the law it upheld permitted "continued confinement of those *already in federal custody* when they could not be safely released." It thus "involved exercise[] of authority derivative of, and in service to, a granted power." But this is a pretty broad understanding of what constitutes a derivative power. If, in the course of exercising an enumerated power, the federal marshals ever take you into custody, they have a derivative power to keep you locked up, forever if necessary.

What actually ends up supplying the determination of what counts as a "great substantive and independent power" is the interpreter's pretheoretical intuitions about which government powers are particularly scary. The Lawson group, in its amicus brief, argues that the authority "to compel private citizens to purchase approved products from other, designated private persons" is "a power truly awesome in scope, and one that, if granted to Congress, the Constitution surely would have enumerated separately."[11] But how do they know?

Roberts's intuitions are most starkly revealed in his attempt to distinguish *Comstock*. The mandate, an obligation to pay money if you impose risks on other people, is an extraordinary power. Locking someone up indefinitely is a mere incident. Here we come to the dark heart of the case against the ACA: the notion that the law's trivial burden on individuals was an intolerable invasion of liberty, "not the country the Framers of our Constitution envisioned," even when the alternative was *really* tough luck for anyone who can't afford medical care.[12]

The joint dissent of Justices Scalia, Kennedy, Thomas, and Alito is no clearer on the Necessary and Proper point. They argue that "one does not regulate commerce that does not exist by compelling its existence," but do not explain why the mandate is not a useful means to the regulation that is authorized. They purport to distinguish *Gonzales v. Raich* on the ground that the prohibition of marijuana cultivation was "the only practicable way" to stop interstate trafficking.

> With the present statute, by contrast, there are many ways other than this unprecedented Individual Mandate by which the regulatory scheme's goals of reducing insurance premiums and ensuring the profitability of insurers could be achieved. For instance, those who did not purchase insurance could be subjected to a surcharge when they do enter the health insurance system. Or they could

be denied a full income tax credit given to those who do purchase the insurance.

So *McCulloch* to the contrary notwithstanding, Congress does not have a choice of means in carrying out its enumerated powers. The Scalia group seems to think that *McCulloch* adopted the rule it specifically rejected: the trouble with the mandate is that it was not *absolutely* necessary. And their support even for this conclusion is weak. When the "regulatory scheme's goals" are enumerated, they omit its overriding one: reducing the number of Americans who have no health insurance. (Later on, they remember this and use it to show that Congress wickedly aimed to force all states to participate in the law's Medicaid expansion.) As we saw in chapter I, the only reason the unpopular mandate got written into the law was that Congress and Obama were both reluctantly convinced, on the basis of extensive analysis by the Congressional Budget Office and outside economists, that there was no other way that the statute could achieve its goals.[13]

What basis have they for rejecting that reasoning? It's impossible to know, because there are no citations to any empirical evidence whatever in the passage just quoted (which I have not edited). In other words, they are ready to destroy a carefully crafted congressional scheme on the basis of their own seat-of-the-pants intuitions about how the world works.

The Scalia group claimed that without the limits they imposed, "then the Commerce Clause becomes a font of unlimited power, or in Hamilton's words, 'the hideous monster whose devouring jaws...spare neither sex nor age, nor high nor low, nor sacred nor profane.'"[14] Roberts had the same concern: "The Commerce Clause is not a general license to regulate an individual from cradle to grave, simply because he will predictably engage in particular transactions." But neither explains why the commerce power is not already sufficiently constrained by *Lopez* and *Morrison*.

The Scalia group went on to vindicate the liberties of those who "have no intention of purchasing most or even any [health care] goods or services and thus no need to buy insurance for those purchases." Justice Ginsburg responded: "[A] healthy young person may be a day away from needing health care." Those who go without health care are not entirely unrelated to that market, any more than drunk drivers are entirely unrelated to other people on the highway. Both are imposing substantial risks on others—in the health care case, the risk of having to pay large amounts for an uninsured person's medical bills.

So the constitutional case against the mandate got five votes—but the statute was nonetheless upheld! Roberts concluded that, although the statute was not authorized under the commerce power, it could be construed to be a tax. Because the judiciary has an obligation to construe a statute in a way that saves its constitutionality if possible—and he was right about that—he concluded that the mandate was a permissible exercise of the taxing power. The payment that is required of those who go without insurance is expected to collect revenue, about $4 billion of it; it is collected by the Internal Revenue Service; it uses factors like those applied to other taxes, such as income level and number of dependents. Unlike penalties, the payment is not limited to willful violations, and the conduct to which the payment applied is not prohibited, but merely conditioned on the payment of money. Since the taxing power is not limited to interstate commerce, the mandate is valid.

The result is ironic. What was so nakedly political about the proposed new Commerce Clause doctrine was that it had so little effect on existing law, and so would not be much of a constraint on Congress in the future. Even Barnett emphasized that the ACA could be invalidated without overturning any New Deal precedents. This was the weapon of a bee: it stings and it dies. Now it's part of constitutional doctrine—Barnett correctly observed afterward that the Court had accepted his arguments,[15] and his views are now enshrined in Commerce Clause jurisprudence—but it doesn't even sting. The new limitations on the Necessary and Proper Clause may be more potent, but it's hard to tell, because they are so vague.

Why are these declamations about the commerce and Necessary and Proper powers in the opinion at all? Roberts explained that he was addressing these issues because the mandate is most naturally read as a regulation of commerce, and only after concluding that it could not be upheld on that ground could he rely on the "saving construction" of deeming the provision a tax. But the modern—that is, post-nineteenth-century!—doctrine of constitutional avoidance holds that judges ought to consider saving constructions *before* addressing constitutional issues, and to try to interpret statutes in a way that allows them to remain silent on the constitutional questions. Justice Brandeis offered the leading formulation in 1936: "When the validity of an act of Congress is drawn in question, and even if a serious doubt of constitutionality is raised, it is a cardinal principle that this Court will first ascertain whether a construction of the statute is fairly possible by which the question may be avoided."[16] Avoidance does not mean deciding the constitutional question and then avoiding it.

This inverted approach to avoidance is particularly surprising coming from Roberts, who has been one of its most energetic practitioners. His Court has been far more reluctant than its predecessor to invalidate laws, and far more likely to creatively construe them to avoid constitutional difficulty. *NFIB v. Sibelius* continues this pattern, but in a curiously roundabout way.

Roberts also placed a new limit on the taxing power. He relied, more heavily than the post–New Deal Court ever had, on *Drexel Furniture*, the child labor tax case. The tax here was constitutional because of several factors that distinguished it from *Drexel*: the penalty was low enough that it "may often be a reasonable financial decision to make the payment rather than purchase insurance." There was no requirement of intent to violate the law, and it was collected through the IRS. It appears that prohibitively high taxes are now constitutionally doubtful, though "we need not here decide the precise point at which an exaction becomes so punitive that the taxing power does not authorize it." Failure to purchase insurance was not treated as an unlawful act; there were no adverse consequences other than the tax. All this is in tension with earlier decisions upholding high taxes, all of which were obviously prohibitory in purpose and effect, on marijuana, sawed-off shotguns, and state-issued banknotes.

Without citation, Roberts appears to have adopted a theory of the tax power developed by Professors Robert Cooter and Neil Siegel. They argue that a law is a tax if it merely dampens the frequency of the taxed conduct, raising revenue, while it is a penalty if it prevents conduct altogether by forcing the actor to pay more than the usual gain from the conduct. They concluded that the ACA mandate is a tax for the same reasons as Roberts. The sum collected is low enough that it will reduce but not eliminate the behavior of going uninsured.[17] But notice what this means, if combined with Roberts's Commerce Clause holding. Recall that one significant concern with the ACA as finally enacted is that Congress made the penalty too small to induce enough people to buy insurance. Roberts now holds that this defect was necessary in order for the law to be constitutionally permissible. If the penalty was large enough that almost everyone was induced to buy insurance, then it would become a penalty.[18] If it actually achieved universal coverage, it would be unconstitutional, because then it would raise no revenue. This may be the most important part of Roberts's holding, though it received almost no attention. It means that a large population of the uninsured is constitutionally *required*. A Tough Luck Constitution.

MEDICAID

The Court's other innovation is its holding that the Medicaid expansion impermissibly pressures the states, because they have no real choice except to acquiesce in the expansion. Roberts thought that states should be able to participate in the old Medicaid program, which covered far fewer people, without joining the new one.

As noted in chapter 2, there were almost no limitations on Congress's spending power after the New Deal. The leading case is *South Dakota v. Dole* (1987), which sustained a law withholding 5% of federal highway funding from states that did not maintain a minimum legal drinking age of twenty-one. The Court warned, however, in a line that Roberts quoted, that financial inducements would be impermissible if they are "so coercive as to pass the point at which 'pressure turns into compulsion.'" These pronouncements never made much sense, which is why they were always ignored before now. They raise deep philosophical questions about what "coercion" is. Clearly, I'm coercing you if I put a gun to your head. But what sense is there in the idea of coercive *offers*? Maybe Esau is coerced if he is so desperately hungry that he will give Jacob anything for some food. But Roberts seems to think that there's coercion any time an offer is *very* generous. If I offer you a million dollars if you'll take off your left shoe and put it back on, I can be pretty sure you'll take my offer, but have I *forced* you? (It may sound silly, but at oral argument, Justice Scalia said that "if you predict... that 100 percent of the States will accept it, that sounds like coercion.") The difference is that in the gun case, you've got a right not to be harmed, but in the shoe case, you have no right to the cash if you keep your shoe on. As Scalia put it in another context, "The reason that denial of participation in a... subsidy scheme does not necessarily 'infringe' a fundamental right is that—unlike direct restriction or prohibition—such a denial does not, as a general rule, have any significant coercive effect."[19] Any subsidy alters financial incentives, but the Court has refused to hold that government decisions to fund childbirth but not abortion coerce women in the exercise of their constitutional rights.

But Roberts declared that denial of future funding "is a gun to the head." Because the program is so big, "over 10 percent of a State's overall budget," it "is economic dragooning that leaves the States with no real option but to acquiesce in the Medicaid expansion."

The reliance on *Dole* was strange. There the state was asserting a right to be free from federal pressure to regulate its own citizens in a way that Congress could not directly require. There was, in this context, some logical sense to the analogy with "unconstitutional conditions," where the state improperly makes individuals give up their constitutional rights in exchange for benefits. Congress could not condition veterans' pensions on an agreement not to criticize the government. Here, however, Congress is regulating the way in which *its own money* is being spent. Medicaid is a program *defined* by its eligibility standards: Congress decrees that people who meet criterion X will get benefit Y. Roberts has given the states the power to revise and edit federal legislation.

States in fact agreed, when they first took Medicaid funding, that Congress was free to modify the program in the future. And as Justice Ginsburg made clear in her opinion, Congress has done that repeatedly. Roberts responds:

> The Medicaid expansion, however, accomplishes a shift in kind, not merely degree. The original program was designed to cover medical services for four particular categories of the needy: the disabled, the blind, the elderly, and needy families with dependent children. Previous amendments to Medicaid eligibility merely altered and expanded the boundaries of these categories. Under the Affordable Care Act, Medicaid is transformed into a program to meet the health care needs of the entire nonelderly population with income below 133 percent of the poverty level. It is no longer a program to care for the neediest among us, but rather an element of a comprehensive national plan to provide universal health insurance coverage.

The logic here turns crucially on the distinction between "the neediest among us" and "the entire nonelderly population with income below 133 percent of the poverty level." Evidently Roberts thinks that if you're merely at the bottom of the income scale, you are not one of the neediest among us. How does he know? Three days earlier, dissenting from a decision invalidating mandatory life without parole for a teenager who participated in a robbery where someone was killed, he declared that the role of judges is not to answer "grave and challenging questions of morality and social policy." But now, he is sure that, as a constitutional matter, the guy who washes the dishes at the restaurant where Roberts eats his lunch, who perhaps is just above the poverty line, and who can't afford to go to the doctor if he starts feeling pains from treatable early-stage cancer, is not among the neediest. Medicaid has for years drawn the line on the basis of a judgment that if adults without children are too poor to pay for medical care, that is their own fault. This was a policy judgment, one that Congress felt free to, and did, reject in the ACA. Now it has become a rule of constitutional law.

How can the preexisting program count as "existing funds" to which the state is entitled? The Medicaid amendment applies *not* to "existing" funds, the funds that states accepted under the terms of earlier versions of Medicaid, but only to the funds the states receive after January 1, 2014.[20] Has the existence of Medicaid somehow restricted the ability of future Congresses to make appropriations? That would contradict "the centuries-old concept that one legislature may not bind the legislative authority of its successors."[21]

What distinguishes a new program from an expansion of an old one? What sense are lower courts, which are supposed to get guidance from the Supreme Court, to make of this new distinction? Justice Ruth Bader Ginsburg suggested that Congress could get around Roberts's new restriction with a law abolishing Medicaid and simultaneously creating a new "Medicaid II" with the same bureaucratic structure but many more beneficiaries.[22] Whatever the practical difficulties of enacting such a measure, its conceded permissibility is devastating to Roberts's logic, because the new program would be exactly as coercive, from the states' point of view, as the provision that he invalidated.

Where is the line to be drawn between inducement and coercion? As with his new limitation of the Necessary and Proper Clause, Roberts does not give us a clue. "We have no need to fix a line.... It is enough for today that wherever that line may be, this statute is surely beyond it." (The deepest mystery about the ACA decision is why Justices Breyer and Kagan, who ought to know better, joined this part of the opinion. At oral argument,

Breyer repeatedly pointed out that the take-it-or-leave-it provision in the Medicaid statute has been there since 1965. Any
explanation is likely to involve interpersonal relationships—if
not an explicit deal, then a friendly gesture toward a chief who
was suddenly very much alone.)

The implications for other federal spending statutes are thus
obscure. The average state receives more than half a billion dollars annually under the two largest federal education grant programs. This money comes with a lot of strings attached, such as
a requirement that the Boy Scouts be given "a fair opportunity
to meet" in the public schools. Probably the most important of
these is Title IX of the Education Amendments of 1972, requiring that equal opportunities be provided to women, which
enabled massive participation in girls' athletics. The long-term
effect of such participation has been more education and higher
incomes for women.[23]

Now consider the Scalia group. They acknowledge that
states are free to refuse money offered by Congress, but note
that "a contract is voidable if coerced." (Relevance doubtful: a
court would not void the contract in my shoe example.) They
reject the government's contention that "neither the amount of
the offered federal funds nor the amount of the federal taxes
extracted from the taxpayers of a State to pay for the program in
question is relevant in determining whether there is impermissible coercion." They explain:

> This argument ignores reality. When a heavy federal tax is
> levied to support a federal program that offers large grants
> to the States, States may, as a practical matter, be unable
> to refuse to participate in the federal program and to sub-
> stitute a state alternative. Even if a State believes that the
> federal program is ineffective and inefficient, withdrawal

would likely force the State to impose a huge tax increase on its residents, and this new state tax would come on top of the federal taxes already paid by residents to support subsidies to participating States.

This has broader implications than they acknowledge. They have not just described the Medicaid expansion. They have described Medicaid itself. As they note, Medicaid is by far the largest federal program of grants to states. Its funding in 2010 exceeded $552 billion, approaching 22% of all state expenditures combined. The new restriction on the spending power would seem to mean that "the sheer size of this federal spending program in relation to state expenditures" makes it unconstitutional, because "a State would be very hard pressed to compensate for the loss of federal funds by cutting other spending or raising additional revenue." It is not clear whether this means that spending programs become unconstitutional, or simply become unrevisable by Congress, when they become a sufficiently large part of a state's budget. There is also a hint that federal taxation itself might violate the Constitution if it is excessive, because "heavy federal taxation diminishes the practical ability of States to collect their own taxes." (They don't mention the Sixteenth Amendment, which on its face gives Congress unlimited power to tax income at any rate it wants.)

The basic difficulty here was noted long ago by the Ninth Circuit, in an analysis that impressed even Judge Vinson:

Does the relevant inquiry turn on how high a percentage of the total programmatic funds is lost when federal aid is cut-off? Or does it turn, as Nevada claims in this case, on what percentage of the federal share is withheld? Or on what percentage of the state's total income would be required to replace those funds? Or on the extent to which alternative private, state, or federal sources of...funding are available? There are other interesting and more fundamental questions. For example, should the fact that Nevada, unlike most states, fails to impose a state income tax on its residents play a part in our analysis? Or, to put the question more basically, can a sovereign state which is always free to increase its tax revenues ever be coerced by the withholding of federal funds—or is the state merely presented with hard political choices?[24]

Neither Roberts nor the Scalia group offered even a hint as to how to answer those questions.

Both justified their reasoning by analogy with the law of contract. A coerced contract is not enforceable. But look what would happen if you tried to apply their approach to an actual contract. Let's imagine that Clarence owns a restaurant and employs Nino as his short-order cook. Nino's job is to cook hamburgers. Their contract is the typical one of employment at will: Nino can quit whenever he wants, and Clarence can fire him whenever *he* wants. The job is Nino's sole source of income; his pay is 100 percent of his household budget. Now Clarence tells Nino that starting next week, grilled cheese sandwiches are added to the menu, and Nino will get a small raise in salary. Nino responds that he hates grilled cheese sandwiches, hates making them, doesn't want to be in the same room with them, and can get by on his old salary. Clarence tells Nino, "Sorry, this is the new menu and the new job. If you can't do what I'm asking, I'll have to get another cook."

If a court used the coercion test newly minted in the ACA case, the result would be an injunction that Clarence must keep paying Nino the "existing funds" he has been getting, and Nino can keep cooking what he has been cooking in the past. (For

Roberts, it evidently would depend on whether the added responsibilities constituted a new job; he would issue the injunction if,
say, the new requirement was that Nino wash Clarence's car.) No
court would rule that way in an actual contract dispute. Clarence
is free to change Nino's prospective job description whenever
and however he likes. But then the analogy to contract law can't
tell you why Congress doesn't have the same freedom.

SEVERABILITY

Most remarkably, the Scalia group wanted to leverage their new
rules into wholesale destruction of the entire statute, the rest of
which was indisputably constitutional. This is the problem of
"severability": if part of a law is unconstitutional, how much of
the rest of the statute has to be struck down as well? The answer
depends on how much of it Congress would have passed had
it known it could not enact the invalid part. The Scalia group
offers an elaborate argument that every last bit of the law is inex-
tricably linked to the two parts that they would invalidate.

They claimed that the statute is an intricately interconnected
structure that is disrupted by even a small change. But the two
changes they proposed to make, striking down the mandate and
making the Medicaid expansion optional for the states, will not
necessarily have any effect at all. They give some regulated entities new options, and everything depends on how those options
are exercised. As the Eleventh Circuit observed, the mandate's
sanction may be too weak, and it may not have much effect at
all on levels of insurance. Other provisions, such as the subsidies
and insurance exchanges, may do more to decrease the number of uninsured. Similarly—and I shall say more about this in
chapter 5—there are enough good reasons for states to accept the

Medicaid expansion that, despite the protestations of a number of governors, they may all end up taking the deal. So the ACA could have ended up operating exactly as intended even without these provisions. The only way that the Scalia group could reach its goal was to assume the worst-case scenario. It's hard to imagine how this novel approach to severability analysis—imagine a conceivable chain reaction in which invalidation frustrates the statutory purpose, and then assume that you know for certain that this will happen—could ever leave anything standing.

The Scalia group was even willing to strike down provisions that they conceded had nothing whatsoever to do with the offensive parts, such as a requirement that chain restaurants display the nutritional content of their food. Here's their argument in full:

> The Court has not previously had occasion to consider severability in the context of an omnibus enactment like the ACA, which includes not only many provisions that are ancillary to its central provisions but also many that are entirely unrelated—hitched on because it was a quick way to get them passed despite opposition, or because their proponents could exact their enactment as the *quid pro quo* for their needed support. When we are confronted with such a so-called "Christmas tree," a law to which many nongermane ornaments have been attached, we think the proper rule must be that when the tree no longer exists the ornaments are superfluous.

In other words, if a legislative scheme has one unconstitutional provision, and some other parts of the scheme will work better if that one is carried out, then the entire law is invalid, including provisions that are entirely unrelated. Severability analysis does not ordinarily mean that a chip in the door jamb brings down the whole structure.

Invalidation of the entire ACA would have produced the most massive disruption that any judicial order had ever brought about in American history. After Judge Vinson, in the early litigation, declared the entire statute unconstitutional, the government filed a motion for clarification, asking what, exactly, he expected to be done. His initial decision was sloppy. He did not follow the normal judicial practice of issuing an injunction specifying whether the government was required to stop operating programs, implementing Medicare reforms, collecting taxes, providing tax credits, and otherwise implementing the statute. The motion (which induced him to stay his ruling pending appeal) observed that, for example, the ACA made many adjustments in Medicare payment rates, and that invalidating the law would require recalculation, with likely consequent delays and errors, of the roughly 100 million Medicare claims that are processed each *month*. Millions of dollars had already been granted to the states to implement their insurance exchanges. If the ACA were invalidated, would the states, which had already spent much of the money, be required to pay it back to the federal government? And what would happen to all the young adults, up to age twenty-six, whose coverage would abruptly be yanked out from under them? The Scalia group's approach raised exactly the same questions, but the judges did not pause to consider them.

Anthony Kennedy has often been regarded as the moderate member of the Court, when he is actually just the swing vote who votes liberal on social issues. Based on his questions during oral argument, I expected him to vote to invalidate the mandate. I was stunned that he was willing to go so far as to try to invalidate the entire law. Moderate is not le *mot juste*. His vote in this case shows a new extremism.

Roberts says that without the new spending power limitations he created, "individual liberty would suffer." Similarly the Scalia group: "The fragmentation of power produced by the structure of our Government is central to liberty, and when we destroy it, we place liberty at peril." Neither specifies how liberty is endangered by the asserted power. Evidently there is a suppressed premise. We can offer an educated guess about what it is: anything that restrains government thereby ipso facto advances liberty. We are back to Tough Luck Libertarianism.

EXPLAINING JOHN ROBERTS

What can we say about why Roberts voted as he did? His opinion is full of sympathy for the challengers, ready to reshape constitutional law in accordance with their vision, but unwilling to consummate the marriage by striking down the law. What was going on?

We get a bit of a clue from an extraordinary leak about the deliberations. The Court's ability to maintain its secrecy has been impressively consistent. Yet three days after the decision was announced, Jan Crawford reported, citing "sources with specific knowledge of the deliberations," that Roberts had initially voted to strike down the mandate but had later changed his mind. Roberts was worried about the lack of existing doctrinal support in the challengers' case. "To strike down the mandate as exceeding the Commerce Clause, the court would have to craft a new theory, which could have opened it up to criticism that it reached out to declare the president's health care law unconstitutional. Roberts was willing to draw that line, but in a way that decided future cases, and not the massive health care case."[25]

There has been plenty of speculation about Roberts's motives. Some of it is too silly to take seriously, for example, that he was intimidated by Obama's inarticulate complaint about judicial activism. (The fact that he changed his mind, if true, reveals nothing about his reasons.) Justice Scalia pointed out the obvious: "What can he do to me? Or to any of us? We have life tenure and we have it precisely so that we will not be influenced by politics, by threats from anybody."[26] The notion that Roberts has gone over to the liberal side of the Court is even sillier: this was the first 5–4 decision ever in which he had sided with the liberals.[27]

A hypothesis that almost nobody was willing to entertain was that Roberts was conscientiously trying to do the best job he could. If that is the case, then the explanation is right there before us, in the text of the opinion he wrote. His opinion is also consistent with broader commitments, to preserving the constitutionality of statutes through saving constructions, that are evident in many of his earlier opinions.[28] That indicates judicial philosophy rather than political calculation.

But there may be a bit more to say. There are some pertinent considerations, not stated in his opinion, and about which he had good reason to be reticent, that could legitimately have influenced his judgment.

New constitutional constructions, of the kind that undergirded the challenge to the mandate, raise deep issues about the appropriate role of the judiciary—issues that go far beyond the health care case. The action/inaction distinction, on which the challenge to the mandate depended, does not appear in the Constitution's text. Nor is it laid down in any precedent. As we have already seen, this is not a fatal objection: there must be construction, and no one can possibly anticipate every construction that a court may devise.

There are, however, two lingering problems, and both of them seem to have troubled Roberts.

One is notice. A basic element of legality is that people should know in advance what their rights are. A long-standing problem with common-law decision making is unfair surprise to the parties. Robert Rantoul complained in 1836 that no one knows what the law is until a judge lays it down, and that this is unjust; "a rule which is unknown can govern no man's conduct."[29] That is particularly a problem in constitutional law, where a legislature may undertake an enormous effort to address a pressing problem, only to be told afterward, on the basis of a newly constructed rule, that what they have done is unconstitutional. It is particularly galling if the constitutional obstacle in question is one that could easily have been navigated around at the time of enactment, and political conditions have meanwhile changed so that the problem can no longer be addressed. The Court's invalidation of anti–Ku Klux Klan legislation in the late 1800s, which several times reversed the convictions of mass murderers on the basis of novel constructions, is a cautionary tale.

The other problem is bias—particularly pressing where there is discretion, as there certainly is when constitutional construction takes place. Barnett recalls a case he prosecuted, at which a judge who normally was strict about the scope of a defendant's cross-examination in a preliminary hearing unexpectedly greatly expanded the scope of cross-examination, over the prosecutors' objection, uncovering surprising information of which the prosecutors had been unaware. "Although we could not prove it, we were convinced that Judge Devine's aberrant behavior (and the police officer's damaging testimony) had been induced by a bribe from the defendant's lawyer."[30] Sometime later, the judge was convicted and sent to prison for multiple instances of corruption. Trial judges routinely make discretionary calls about the evidence that is admissible. But that has its dangers.

In constitutional law, the Supreme Court necessarily gets to create new constitutional rules. But the problems of notice and bias, taken together, present unpleasant possibilities.

Professors Jack Balkin and Sanford Levinson have distinguished two senses in which constitutional law decisions can be political. "High politics," in which judges promote broad political principles, inevitably influence constitutional law. Construction is guided by one's broad interpretation of the Constitution's purposes, and that in turn is likely to be influenced by one's overall political vision. Because different Americans have different visions, conflict at this level is inevitable. That's why it matters so much who gets appointed to the Supreme Court. What is improper is the influence of "low politics," in which judges aim at short-term advantage for the political party that they favor.[31] The danger here is what happened in *Bush v. Gore*: the courts will use their discretion in a way that favors their political friends. When they do that, the difference between them and Judge Devine is one of degree and not of kind. It is a corruption of the judicial process if the Supreme Court fabricates new rules just to help the Republicans.

Doubtless the four dissenters did not consciously mean to do that, but people can deceive themselves about their own motives. Isn't it odd that the mandate, which a few years earlier was the Republican alternative to Clinton's health plan, suddenly became, once Obama supported it, a tyrannical violation of a new, unenumerated liberty? May we not suspect that, if Obama had rejected the mandate and chosen a different mechanism, those wonderfully creative Republicans would have invented a different constitutional rule, which *that* mechanism would have violated?

This creates a problem for the conscientious judge. If I get to make new rules that just happen to be politically convenient, how can I (much less everyone watching me) know that I have not become a corrupt political tool? (The liberals on the Court didn't have this problem, because, as Ginsburg's dissent made clear, the ACA can easily be upheld by straightforwardly applying long-standing law. No invention is necessary.)

It is a rule of law, not merely a prudential bit of advice, that judges should avoid even the appearance of a conflict of interest. That can't rule out high politics, for reasons I've already explained, but it obviously applies to low politics. Roberts was right to worry. The low-political dimensions of the case put him in an awkward position. The Scalia group made his problem worse by insisting that the entire law, not just the health care mandate, needed to be struck down. Roberts feared, perhaps, that the Court would be perceived as having done something shameful. The four dissenters appear to be incapable of shame.

Barnett's vision of the Constitution evidently struck a chord in the heart of John Roberts. His opinion is full of enthusiasm for it. But at the same time, perhaps he worried about the too-convenient result. How could he possibly prove to the world—and, perhaps, to himself as well—that he was not merely a low politician? His solution: lay down Barnett's rule for the future, but find a way to keep it from producing a low-political payoff in this case. (With the Medicaid provision, he at least had dicta about coercive conditions to rely on.)[32] That way the high-politics holding is purged of the suspicion of low politics. No wonder he is being reviled by those who don't understand the difference.

Crawford reports that "it was clear to the conservatives that Roberts wanted the court out of the red-hot dispute." Ordinarily, in cases where a judge's impartiality reasonably can be questioned, the remedy is recusal: the judge simply takes himself off the case. But that wasn't a possibility here: every member of the Court had low-politics skin in the game, and the Court had to hear the case because the Eleventh Circuit had struck down the mandate. So what to do? The answer, perhaps, is that the argument for the convenient outcome has to be unusually compelling, so that it will be clear to everyone that low-political bias isn't doing the work—and Roberts rightly concluded that this challenge did not meet that standard.

FIVE

Where It Hurts

So what were the consequences of the Court's decision? Ordinarily we would begin by discussing how the decision changed the law. But on this issue, it is hard to say much. As we have seen, there are now vague new limits on the Congress's power to regulate commerce, on the Necessary and Proper Clause, on the taxing power, and on the spending power. The Court wrote itself a lot of blank checks. How it fills them in will depend on elections and retirements. If there are more conservatives on the Court, then these may be potent. If there are more liberals, these limits are likely to be forgotten.

The most important consequence, of course, is that the ACA was not strangled in the cradle. The law's effects unfold at a glacial pace: the Medicaid expansion, and the state-based insurance exchanges with large subsidies for those making up to 400% of the poverty level, commence in 2014. So does the mandate. Exclusions for preexisting conditions will end. So will annual and lifetime limits on coverage, which deprive people of support when their medical expenses are highest. Small businesses with low-wage workers will receive tax credits to help with their contributions to employees' premiums. The cost of buying insurance in the individual market will drop nearly 60 percent by 2016. For those in small groups such as small businesses, premiums will decline by around 10 percent.[1] Medicare recipients will see growing reductions in the cost of their medications, as well as better and more coordinated primary care, reducing costs at the same time that it provides higher quality care. Young adults already can stay on their parents' insurance policies until age twenty-six, and when they are older, so long as their wages are low, they will be eligible for Medicaid. Even families making more than $250,000 a year, whose taxes will rise by nearly 1%, will benefit from the end of caps on coverage, and they will no longer be at risk of losing their policies if they get sick. The ACA also puts in place a number of pilot programs of promising but untested ideas for reducing cost and improving quality. There are dozens of other small adjustments to the American health care delivery system. The law is not easily summarized.

If the dissenters had their way, none of this would have happened. The longer the law remains in place, the more constituents will discover that it does things that they like. The huge political blunder of the ACA was that it was implemented so slowly that few of the beneficiaries were aware of what they were being given until long after passage, and in the meantime the Democrats paid a hefty price for enacting the bill, notably the loss of the House in the 2010 elections. Time will cure that. If the ACA survives its first few years, it will become politically untouchable, like Social Security and Medicare.

The most important question, after the Supreme Court's intervention, is the fate of the Medicaid expansion. The other long-term question is the future of Tough Luck Libertarianism.

SO WHAT HAPPENS TO THE
MEDICAID EXPANSION?

The Court ruled that the states could turn down the Medicaid expansion while continuing to participate in the old Medicaid program. One might have expected that no state would turn down such a good deal: the federal government will pick up 100 percent of the costs until 2016, with its contribution gradually declining to 90 percent in 2020 and thereafter. And there is added pressure to take the money, because previous forms of federal aid were cut off. Hospital associations agreed to accept cuts to their reimbursement rates, expecting that this would be more than made up by money from patients newly insured through Medicaid. States refusing the money would not only be hurting their own working poor and local hospitals, the largest employer in many counties. They'd be rejecting a huge infusion of cash into their economies, creating many, many jobs—good jobs, for doctors and well-paid medical technicians. That money has a powerful multiplier effect, creating jobs outside the health sector as well.[2]

Yet in the weeks after the Court's decision, a number of governors announced that they would turn down the money, and others were noncommittal. This opposition was not purely partisan (though it obviously had a partisan element): at least seven Democratic governors were among the uncertain ones. "Unlike the federal government, Montana can't just print money," said Governor Brian Schweitzer, a Democrat. "We have a budget surplus, and we're going to keep it that way."[3]

Schweitzer's concerns are legitimate. The ACA was enacted during an economic recession that hit state budgets hard, forcing cutbacks in education, roads, police, prisons, and public services. In particular, Medicaid growth has tended to accompany cuts in education aid.[4] It's the worst time for the states to be required to spend more money—even the relatively low contribution they would have to make after 2020.

States are presently under pressure to keep their taxes down, because if they do not, they will be at a competitive disadvantage with other states. The ACA evidently regarded this as a race to the bottom, which it aimed to forestall by bribing all states into the system. If all states could raise their taxes together, then there would be enough money for both health care and education. That race was revived when the Supreme Court intervened to break up the bribe into smaller pieces, some of which are easier to refuse. States habitually worry about that.

Yet any savings by nonparticipation is a false economy. Consider Texas, by far the biggest prize in this fight. One in four Texans is uninsured. The ACA would insure almost 2 million of them. The expansion would give Texas an additional $52.5 billion from 2014 to 2019, which is more than half of the state's annual budget.[5] As noted in the introduction, lack of insurance is a public health disaster; the Medicaid expansion means that people will live who would otherwise die.

Yet Governor Rick Perry announced that he would refuse the money. "Medicaid is a system of inflexible mandates, one-size-fits-all requirements, and wasteful, bureaucratic inefficiencies. Expanding it as the PPACA provides would only exacerbate the failure of the current system, and would threaten even Texas with financial ruin."[6] So what will happen to those in Texas without insurance? "Every Texan has health care in this state," Perry told Fox News. "From the standpoint of being able to have access to health care, every Texan has that. How we pay for it and how we deliver it should be our decision, not some bureaucrat in Washington, D.C., that may have never been to Texas a day in their life or, for that matter, in any of the other 49 states, trying to mandate this one-size-fits-all health care."[7] This is Tinkerbell again. In Texas, adults who are not disabled or elderly are eligible for Medicaid only if they have children, and even then only if their incomes are less than 23 percent of the poverty level. Perry is saying, in essence, that Texas's health care system is already fine, and no additional dollars are necessary. (Perry had previously considered dropping out of Medicaid altogether, casting doubt on the claim that the program is an offer the states can't refuse.)[8] Yet four days before Perry announced his decision, the federal Agency for Healthcare Research and Quality ranked Texas as having the worst health care in the nation.[9] A few weeks later, the *New England Journal of Medicine* reported that Medicaid significantly reduces mortality.[10] A study by the Perryman Group, a financial analysis firm, found that every dollar spent by Texas would produce $1.29 in tax revenue."[11] It's hard to get a coherent story out of Perry's statements, which are a disjointed collection of slogans, like the things the bad guys say in *Atlas Shrugged*.

The most sophisticated case for states turning down the money was developed by Douglas Holtz-Eakin, former Congressional Budget Office director. Because any individual who is above the federal poverty line (up to 400%) is eligible for subsidies in the state-based insurance exchanges, and states do not have to contribute anything to help insure those people, states have an incentive to shift that population out of Medicaid. Refusing the Medicaid expansion does that. "Everybody between 100 percent and 133 percent would be eligible for insurance subsidies—with the federal government (read: taxpayer) picking up the entire tab."[12] The consequence would be an explosion of federal costs.

Holtz-Eakin presupposes, however, that the entire population above the poverty line will in fact buy insurance on the exchanges. These people have very little money, and many of them are likely to forgo even subsidized insurance. That's why the ACA added them to Medicaid. (Because Medicaid is free, poverty doesn't deter people from signing up for it.) So much of this population is likely to remain uninsured and end up getting care they cannot pay for, with results much more expensive than if the state had simply chipped in 10 percent of their Medicaid costs. Holtz-Eakin's analysis also presupposed that states would have the option of accepting the Medicaid expansion in part, covering only those below the poverty line. Obama made clear in December 2012 that this isn't an option: if states want the expansion, they have to accept all of it.

This analysis is reinforced by a July 2012 analysis by the Congressional Budget Office of the likely economic consequences of the Supreme Court's decision. The CBO estimated that about half of the people who are uninsured because states decline the Medicaid expansion will get their insurance through the exchanges. About 3 million fewer people will be covered, saving the federal government about $84 billion from 2012 to 2022.[13]

This is not such a good deal for the states. Instead of paying 10 percent of the cost for, let's say, 100,000 people, a state will pay 100 percent of the cost of uncompensated care for the 50,000 who will not end up in the exchanges. Even the subsidies have a downside. Employers are not liable for penalties if their employees receive Medicaid; they are if employees get federal subsidies for insurance. So if states pursue this strategy, they will hurt employers of low-wage workers, and penalize job creation. Joey Fishkin suggests that it is a shame that the Court couldn't get the CBO to score its proposal before it enacted it.[14]

There was resistance to the original Medicaid program, which also demanded state contributions, but rewarded them with a large infusion of federal money. Only slightly more than half the states implemented a Medicaid program in the first year that federal funding was available. Within four years, nearly all had done so.[15]

The Obama strategy, which may yet be vindicated, is to duplicate Roosevelt's achievement with Social Security and Johnson's with Medicare: creating such a huge constituency of beneficiaries for the new federal program that it is politically impossible to abolish it, permanently establishing a regime with higher taxes and more economic and physical security for those at the bottom. The Court's intervention may end up making that more expensive, and the program will certainly have to be tweaked to address cost problems, as has happened with both Social Security and Medicare. But if it works, then the American social contract will thereafter proceed on a fundamentally different basis than before.

YOUR TOUGH LUCK

There is another way—the way of Tough Luck Libertarianism. An uninsured population will impose costs on Texas if and only if Texas feels obligated to provide them with medical care. As we saw in the introduction, Justice Scalia has a solution: don't obligate yourself to that. You can tell hospitals—Governor Perry is in effect telling them—that they just have to absorb the federal spending cuts, and that no further money will come from the state. That will lead some hospitals to close and others to cut back on uncompensated care. People who can't afford medical care will have to do without. Representative Phil Gingrey of Georgia urged his governor to reject the Medicaid expansion. When he was asked what the 500,000 people in his state who would thus be deprived of insurance are supposed to do, he replied that those at that income level have "got a little bit

more money in their pocket than those who are at 100 percent
of the federal poverty level."[16] A great comfort if they get cancer. (Gingrey actually misstates the preexisting rules in Georgia,
where working parents are eligible only if their incomes do not
exceed 50 percent of the poverty level, or about $9,500 for a
family of three, while adults without dependent children are not
eligible at any income level.)

Political warfare evidently produces collateral damage.
Obama owns the health care bill, so anything that can gum up
its works is a Republican victory—and almost all the state challengers were Republicans. But all those working poor people are
not Democratic party operatives. They are ordinary folk trying
to get by. Response to political incentives once again begets an
alliance with Tough Luck Libertarianism.

Poor and helpless people are unlikely to get much in
American politics unless their interests are in some ways tied to
those of the wealthy and powerful. (The agricultural industry's
support for food stamps is the reason there isn't much outright
starvation in America.) Hospitals that provide uncompensated
care badly need that federal money. If you are a hospital executive in Texas, you probably have a fiduciary duty to do all you
can to defeat Rick Perry.

The Affordable Care Act remains controversial. After the
Court's decision, the House, controlled by the Republicans,
voted to repeal it. Their slogan is "repeal and replace," but no
replacement was offered.[17] There are elements in the Republican
Party that seriously hope to reform the medical care system
on market-based lines. Representative Paul Ryan showed real
political courage in proposing radical changes in Medicare
and Medicaid (changes that I think would be destructive, but
this is an honest policy disagreement), though he was forced to

backpedal hard on Medicare after he became Mitt Romney's running mate in the 2012 presidential campaign. But the fact that Ryan and other reformers must contend with is that there is just not much interest within the Republican coalition in taking on the health care issue.

In 2012, the ACA survived mortal danger twice. The first was the constitutional challenge. The second was the presidential election. Romney pledged that, if elected, he would immediately waive its requirements by executive order, and then work to repeal it. It is unclear whether he had the power to do that, but it is clear that the president has the authority to disrupt the operation of the statute in countless ways. Obama's reelection ensures that the law will be implemented as intended. If a Republican president is elected in 2016, that person will find a law that is much harder to dismantle, with health exchanges operating in every state and millions of people relying for their health care on the insurance that the statute provides.

Eventually, perhaps the ACA will lose its political salience and become a familiar and uninteresting part of the landscape. The passion with which it is opposed is tightly connected with Republican Party imperatives. Once Obama leaves office, the partisan impulse will fade. Only naked Tough Luck Libertarianism will remain. As I noted in the introduction, almost no one really is a tough luck libertarian. That philosophy is effective only when it is allied with other political forces.

But the law may not survive. I may be underestimating the durability of the opposition. And for reasons already reviewed, if it dies, it is likely that nothing will be put in its place. To that extent, even if no one overtly avows Tough Luck Libertarianism, the United States will become a Tough Luck Libertarian nation. Hobbes thought that even the strongest person would have conclusive reason to want to leave the state of nature, because everyone has to sleep sometime; no one is safe in a condition of anarchy. Everyone gets old and sick, too, and children may not share their parents' economic status. The tough luck of all those who are going to lose their health insurance, if the ACA's opponents prevail, may be your tough luck too.

Notes

Introduction

1. Transcript of Oral Argument, Dept. of Health and Human Services v. Florida (No. 11-398), Supreme Court of the United States, Mar. 27, 2012. I will not give specific page citations to this or to the Court's decision, since these are easily available in computer-searchable sources.
2. See video at http://www.cnn.com/video/?/video/crime/2012/03/27/nr-toobin-mandate.cnn#/video/crime/2012/03/27/nr-toobin-mandate.cnn.
3. Patient Protection and Affordable Care Act, Pub. L. No. 111-148, 124 Stat. 119 (2010), *amended by* Health Care and Education Reconciliation Act of 2010, Pub. L. No. 111-152, 124 Stat. 1029. The specific provision is § 1501(b), 124 Stat. at 244 (codified at 26 U.S.C. § 5000A).
4. United States Government Accountability Office, Private Health Insurance: Estimates of Individuals with Pre-existing Conditions Range from 36 Million to 122 Million (March 2012).
5. John E. McDonough, Inside National Health Reform 120 (2011).
6. A bit later, Alito said: "Are you denying this? If you took the group of people who are subject to the mandate and you calculated the amount of health care services this whole group would consume and figured out the cost of an insurance policy

to cover the services that group would consume, the cost of that policy would be much, much less than the kind of policy that these people are now going to be required to purchase under the Affordable Care Act?"

7. If it is an ordinary commodity, it should be distributed to those whose preferences, as revealed by their willingness to pay, indicate the strongest desire for it. Uwe Reinhardt illustrates the point by imagining two families, a rich family with a healthy baby and a poor family with a sick baby. In an unregulated market, the healthy baby is likely to have more pediatric visits. By the metric of willingness to pay, this is an efficient outcome, and it would be inefficient to shift medical resources to the poor, sick baby. Uwe Reinhardt, *Foreword*, in T. E. Rice, The Economics of Health Reconsidered xiv–xv (2d ed. 2003).

8. Paul Starr, Remedy and Reaction: The Peculiar American Struggle over Health Care Reform 153 (2011).

9. One reason that the for-profit insurance companies were reluctant to support the Obama plan was that risk selection—that is, devising clever ways to keep the sick off their rolls—was what they knew how to do, and under the new law they would not be able to do it anymore. Starr, Remedy and Reaction 219. No rich country in the world other than the United States allows health insurance to be administered by for-profit companies. T. R. Reid, The Healing of America: A Global Quest for Better, Cheaper, and Fairer Health Care 235–36 (2009).

10. This is not a right to all possible health care, since resource scarcity exists and "rationing" in some form is unavoidable. It means a right to a basic level of health care for everyone, at a level that society can afford to pay for. I do not claim that this is a positive right under the U.S. Constitution. I follow Jeremy Waldron (The Right to Private Property (1988), 25): "[A]n argument counts as right-based just in case it takes the moral importance of some individual interest as a reason for assigning duties or imposing moral requirements." If the United States could reduce deaths from curable illness to the average rate of the three top-performing countries, there would be about 100,000 fewer deaths per year.

Ellen Nolte & C. Martin McKee, *Measuring the Health of Nations: Updating an Earlier Analysis*, Health Affairs, Jan./Feb. 2008, 71.

11. Lawrence R. Jacobs & Theda Skocpol, Health Care Reform and American Politics: What Everyone Needs to Know 20 (2010).

12. Stuart Altman & David Shactman, Power, Politics, and Universal Health Care 11–12 (2011); Institute of Medicine, Care Without Coverage: Too Little, Too Late (2002).

13. John Z. Ayanian et al., *The Relation Between Health Insurance Coverage and Clinical Outcomes among Women with Breast Cancer*, 1993 New Eng. J. Medicine 326.

14. Stan Dorn, Urban Inst., Uninsured and Dying Because of It: Updating the Institute of Medicine Analysis on the Impact of Uninsurance on Mortality 3 (2008); Andrew Wilper et al., *Health Insurance and Mortality in US Adults*, 99 Am. J. Pub. Health 2289 (2009).

15. Starr, Remedy and Reaction 242.

16. John Rawls, A Theory of Justice (1971; revised ed. 1999).

17. John Rawls, Justice as Fairness: A Restatement 174 (2001). As I argue in chapter 3, one can derive a similar conclusion from Locke.

18. Robert Nozick, Anarchy, State, and Utopia (1974).

19. George Kateb, *The Night Watchman State*, 45 Am. Scholar 816, 824–25 (Winter 1975–76).

20. Philip Rucker, *Sen. DeMint of S.C. Is Voice of Opposition to Health-Care Reform*, Wash. Post, July 28, 2009.

21. On the specific flaws of Nozick's critique of Rawls, see Thomas W. Pogge, John Rawls 178–84 (2007). The weaknesses of libertarianism are further explored in Andrew Koppelman with Tobias Barrington Wolff, A Right to Discriminate? How the Case of *Boy Scouts of America v. James Dale* Warped the Law of Free Association (2009).

22. Nozick, Anarchy, State, and Utopia 235.

23. See John Tomasi, Free Market Fairness 151–61 (2012).

24. He bills his position as Kantian, but Kant's actual views are closer to those of Rawls. See Allen D. Rosen, Kant's Theory of Justice 173–208 (1993).

25. See http://volokh.com/2011/02/15/asteroid-defense-and-libertarianism/ (Feb. 15, 2011).

26. http://www.mediaite.com/tv/cnntea-party-debate-audience-cheers-letting-uninsured-comatose-man-die/.

27. Transcribed from the broadcast performance of *Peter Pan* (with Mary Martin as Peter), Dec. 8, 1960, at approximately 1:15, http://archives.museum.tv/archives. The episode occurs in the original novel but is less effective there.

28. Remarks to the Greater Cleveland Partnership and a Question-and-Answer Session in Cleveland, Ohio, 43 Weekly Comp. Pres. Doc. 922 (July 10, 2007).

29. See Jonathan Cohn, Sick: The Untold Story of America's Health Care Crisis and the People Who Pay the Price ix–xiv (2007). In fairness, when you read the remark in context, Bush seems to be clumsily trying to call attention to the inefficiency of this approach.

30. David Dranove, Code Red: An Economist Explains How to Revive the Healthcare System Without Destroying It 9 (2008); U.S. Department of Health and Human Services, Centers for Medicare and Medicaid Services, Table 1: National Health Expenditure Aggregate, http://www.cms.gov/National-HealthExpendData/downloads/tables.pdf.

31. On the inevitable inadequacy of private charity, see Cohn, Sick 143–65.

32. See Timothy Stoltzfus Jost, Health Care at Risk: A Critique of the Consumer-Driven Movement (2007). For a critique of the ACA from a consumer-driven perspective (coauthored by one of the earliest defenders of an individual mandate!), see Grace-Marie Turner, James C. Capretta, Thomas P. Miller, & Robert E. Moffit, Why Obamacare Is Wrong for America (2011).

Chapter 1   *The Road to the Mandate*

1. Quoted in Stuart Altman & David Shactman, Power, Politics, and Universal Health Care 103 (2011).

2. Einer Elhauge, *If Health Insurance Mandates Are Unconstitutional, Why Did the Founding Fathers Back Them?*, New Republic Online, Apr. 13, 2012, http://www.tnr.com/article/politics/102620/individual-mandate-history-affordable-care-act.

3. Howard M. Leichner, A Comparative Approach to Policy Analysis: Health Care Policy in Four Nations 121–24 (1979).

4. Starr, Remedy and Reaction 36–37; Cohn, Sick 7–8, 31–34.

5. Cohn, Sick 8.

6. Altman & Shactman 124–25.

7. Starr, Remedy and Reaction 42; Altman 101.

8. Jost, Health Care at Risk 59–61.

9. Health Insurance Association of America, Source Book of Health Insurance Data 39 (2000).

10. Jacobs & Skocpol 135.

11. Altman & Shactman 103.

12. *Id.*, 104.

13. An invaluable corrective here is Steven Croley's careful delineation of the political dynamics of federal administration (and devastating critique of the public choice theory) in Regulation and Public Interests (2008).

14. Paul Starr, The Social Transformation of American Medicine 272 (1982).

15. Altman & Shactman 122–23.

16. *Id.*, 128.

17. *Id.*, 104.

18. *Id.*, 114–15.

19. *Id.*, 116–21.

20. *Id.*, 106–07.

21. *Id.*, 127.

22. Starr, Remedy and Reaction 45.

23. Altman & Shactman 129.

24. Theodore Marmor, The Politics of Medicare 13 (2d ed. 2000).

25. Cohn, Sick 92.

26. Marmor 13.

27. U.S. Census Bureau, *Poverty Status of People by Age, Race, and Hispanic Origin   1959–2010,* http://www.census.gov/hhes/www/poverty/data/historical/people.html.

28. Altman & Shactman 141.

29. Starr, Remedy and Reaction 46–47.

30. Alabama Medicaid Agency, A Medicaid Primer (Jan. 2010), at 7; Jacobs & Skocpol 92.
31. Starr, Remedy and Reaction 52–58.
32. *Id.*, 58.
33. Dranove 97.
34. U.S. Department of Health and Human Services, New Data Say Uninsured Account for Nearly One-Fifth of Emergency Room Visits, July 15, 2009, http://www.hhs.gov/news/press/2009pres/07/20090715b.html.
35. Starr, Remedy and Reaction 27.
36. U.S. Department of Health and Human Services, Centers for Medicare and Medicaid Services, Table 1: National Health Expenditure Aggregate, http://www.cms.gov/NationalHealthExpendData/downloads/tables.pdf.
37. Starr, Remedy and Reaction 72.
38. Altman & Shactman 229.
39. National Health Expenditure Aggregate, supra, Table 1.
40. Reid 20–21.
41. Starr, Remedy and Reaction 73.
42. *Id.*, 2.
43. Altman & Shactman 94.
44. Starr, Remedy and Reaction 108.
45. Altman & Shactman 92.
46. Quoted in Haynes Johnson & David S. Broder, The System: The American Way of Politics at the Breaking Point 234 (1996).
47. Altman & Shactman 93.
48. *Id.*, 191, 198.
49. Jacobs & Skocpol 30–31.
50. Cohn 24–25.
51. Starr, Remedy and Reaction 13, 155; Jared Bernstein & Elise Gould, *Economic Indicators: Income Picture, August 29, 2006*, Economic Policy Institute, at http://www.epi.org/publications/entry/webfeatures_econindicators_income20060829/.
52. Starr, Remedy and Reaction 156.
53. Cohn 10.
54. Jacobs & Skocpol 44.

55. Theda Skocpol & Vanessa Williamson, The Tea Party and the Remaking of Republican Conservatism (2012).

56. Starr, Remedy and Reaction 122–23, 237.

57. Michael T. Doonan & Katharine R. Tull, *Health Care Reform in Massachusetts: Implementation of Coverage Expansions and a Health Insurance Mandate*, 88 MILBANK Q. 54, 70 (2010).

58. A short and clear introduction is Jonathan Gruber, Health Care Reform: What It Is, Why It's Necessary, How It Works (2011). For more detailed accounts, see Staff of the Washington Post, Landmark: The Inside Story of America's New Health-Care Law and What It Means for Us All (2010); Jacobs & Skocpol 121–46; and John E. McDonough, Inside National Health Reform (2011).

59. Altman & Shactman 327.

60. Jacobs & Skocpol 127.

61. Letter from Douglas Elmendorf, Director, Congressional Budget Office, to Hon. Nancy Pelosi, Mar. 20, 2010, http://www.cbo.gov/sites/default/files/cbofiles/ftpdocs/113xx/doc11379/amendreconprop.pdf. After the Supreme Court's decision, the CBO revised its estimate to include an additional $84 billion in savings, because some states would decline the Medicaid expansion. It is uncertain, however, that these states will stay out of the program. See chapter 5.

62. See Stephanie Woolhandler & David Himmelstein, *Healthcare Reform 2.0*, 78 Soc. Research 719 (2011).

63. 42 U.S.C. §§ 300gg, 300gg-1(a), 300gg-3(a).

64. Stuart M. Butler, Assuring Affordable Health Care for All Americans, Heritage Foundation, 1989, http://healthcarereform.procon.org/sourcefiles/1989_assuring_affordable_health_care_for_all_americans.pdf; Mark V. Pauly, Patricia Damon, Paul Feldstein, & John Hoff, *A Plan for Responsible National Health Insurance*, 10 Health Affairs 5 (1991).

65. Robert E. Moffitt, *Personal Freedom, Responsibility, and Mandates*, 13 Health Affairs 101 (1994).

66. John A. Graves & Sharon K. Long, Why Do People Lack Health Insurance?, Urban Institute, 2006.

67. All this history from Paul Starr, *The Mandate Miscalculation*, New Republic Online, Dec. 14, 2011.

68. Starr, Remedy and Reaction 186.

69. *Id.*, 187.

70. *Id.*

71. Ron Suskind, Confidence Men 263 (2011), reports that Obama "was concerned about legal challenges to it." There is no further explanation of the "legal challenges" that Obama anticipated.

72. Tom Daschle with David Nather, Getting It Done: How Obama and Congress Finally Broke the Stalemate to Make Way for Health Care Reform 152, 187 (2010); Letter of Douglas Elmendorf, Director, Congressional Budget Office, to Rep. Bruce Braley, Dec. 29, 2009, http://www.cbo.gov/sites/default/files/cbofiles/ftpdocs/108xx/doc10872/12-29-tort_reform-braley.pdf.

73. A few outlier Republicans, such as Senator Olympia Snowe, might have supported the law, but after many discussions majority leader Harry Reid could not pin her down on what it would take to get her vote. Daschle, Getting It Done 220.

74. Starr, *The Mandate Miscalculation*. The CBO has recently reaffirmed its earlier analysis. Congressional Budget Office, Reducing the Deficit: Spending and Revenue Options 199–200 (Mar. 2011), http://www.cbo.gov/sites/default/files/cbofiles/ftpdocs/120xx/doc12085/03-10-reducingthedeficit.pdf.

75. Affordable Health Care for America Act, H.R. 3962, 111th Cong., 1st Sess., §501 (2009).

76. America's Healthy Future Act of 2009, S. 1796, 111th Cong., 1st Sess., §1301.

77. Reid 88, 179.

78. McDonough 122.

79. Jonathan Gruber, *Health Care Reform Without the Individual Mandate: Replacing the Individual Mandate Would Significantly Erode Coverage Gains and Raise Premiums for Health Care Customers*, Ctr. for Am. Progress 3–5 (Feb. 2011), http://www.americanprogress.org/issues/2011/02/pdf/gruber_mandate.pdf. That analysis is reasonably contestable, since any analysis depends on educated guesses about how people will behave. For a strong argument in favor of the opt-out option, see Starr, *The Mandate Miscalculation*.

Chapter 2 *Appropriate Constitutional Limits*

1. Cf. Gary Lawson, *On Reading Recipes . . . and Constitutions*, 85 Geo. L.J. 1823 (1997). The analogy is better with Shakespeare than with most other playwrights, since Shakespeare did not authorize publication of any of his plays in his lifetime. His scripts were strictly instructions for performance.

2. 2 Records of Fed. Convention 21 (Max Farrand ed., 1911); *see also* 1 *id.* 21 (Resolution VI of the Virginia Plan).

3. Oxford English Dictionary, "Subsidiarity" (2d ed. 1989).

4. Robert K. Vischer, *Subsidiarity as a Principle of Governance: Beyond Devolution*, 35 Ind. L. Rev. 103, 142 (2001). Another basis for intervention by the center—one authorized by the Civil War Amendments, which I will discuss shortly—is the protection of human rights, which states may disregard even in the absence of any collective action problem. Some have argued that health care is such a right. I will not pursue that argument here.

5. Jack M. Balkin, Living Originalism 145 (2011).

6. Compare *id.* 138–82 with Randy E. Barnett, *Jack Balkin's Interaction Theory of "Commerce,"* 2012 U. Ill. L. Rev. 623.

7. Gibbons v. Ogden, 22 U.S. (9 Wheat.) 1, 194 (1824); Balkin 140, 160–62. Some Republicans still advocate this understanding of the commerce power. *See, e.g.,* Steven G. Calabresi & Nicholas Terrell, *The Number of States and the Economics of American Federalism*, 63 Fla. L. Rev. 1, 6 (2011) ("The most compelling argument in American history for empowering our national government has been the need to overcome collective action problems."); Steven G. Calabresi, *"A Government of Limited and Enumerated Powers": In Defense of* United States v. Lopez, 94 Mich. L. Rev. 752, 786 (1995) (noting importance of collective action problems). The most rigorously worked out defense of this reading of the Commerce Clause is Robert D. Cooter & Neil S. Siegel, *Collective Action Federalism: A General Theory of Article I, Section 8*, 63 Stan. L. Rev. 115 (2010). See also Donald H. Regan, *How to Think About the Federal Commerce Power and Incidentally Rewrite* United States v. Lopez, 94 Mich. L. Rev. 554 (1995); Robert L. Stern, *The Commerce That Concerns More States Than One*, 47 Harv. L. Rev. 1335 (1934).

8. Stern 1335.
9. See the comparative data in Donald S. Lutz, *Toward a Theory of Constitutional Amendment*, in Responding to Imperfection: The Theory and Practice of Constitutional Amendment 261 (Sanford Levinson ed. 1995).
10. U.S. CONST. art. 1, § 8.
11. 17 U.S. (4 Wheat.) 316 (1819).
12. Opinion on the Constitutionality of a Bill for Establishing a National Bank, in 19 Papers of Thomas Jefferson 275, 279 (1974).
13. 130 S.Ct. 1949 (2010).
14. Gibbons v. Ogden, 22 U.S. (9 Wheat.) 1, 195 (1824).
15. Slaughterhouse Cases, 83 U.S. (16 Wall.) 36 (1873).
16. 92 U.S. 542 (1876).
17. Quoted in Barry Friedman, The Will of the People 144 (2009).
18. Leonard W. Levy, *United States v. Cruikshank*, in Encyclopedia of the American Constitution 733 (Leonard W. Levy & Kenneth L. Karst eds. 2000).
19. 203 U.S. 1 (1906).
20. Pamela S. Karlan, *Contracting the Thirteenth Amendment:* Hodges v. United States, 85 B.U. L. Rev. 783, 807 (2005).
21. See Pamela Brandwein, Rethinking the Judicial Settlement of Reconstruction (2011).
22. 198 U.S. 45 (1905).
23. See William E. Forbath, Law and the Shaping of the American Labor Movement (1991); William E. Forbath, *Courts, Constitutions, and Labor Politics in England and America: A Study of the Constitutive Power of Law*, 16 L. & Soc. Inquiry 1 (1991).
24. Lucas County v. State of Ohio, 75 O.S. 131 (1906).
25. Coppage v. Kansas, 236 U.S. 1, 17 (1915).
26. Hugh D. Hindman, Child Labor: An American History 49 (2002).
27. *Id.* 55–59; Stephen B. Wood, Constitutional Politics in the Progressive Era: Child Labor and the Law 9, 25, 39 (1968).
28. Wood 32–33, 295; William Graebner, *Federalism in the Progressive Era: A Structural Interpretation of Reform*, 64 J. Am. Hist. 331, 335–37 (1977).
29. Wood 56, 77.

30. Hammer v. Dagenhart, 247 U.S. 251, 256–57 (1918).
31. *Id.*, 276.
32. Wood 169–219, 255–99.
33. Quoted in *id.*, 295.
34. Hindman 68.
35. United States v. Darby, 312 U.S. 100, 115–17 (1941).
36. 317 U.S. 111 (1942).
37. John Jeffries, later the dean of the University of Virginia School of Law.
38. See 1 Laurence H. Tribe, American Constitutional Law 913–14 (3d ed. 2000).
39. There were no available national statistics on poverty among the elderly in the mid-1930s, but the Social Security Administration summarized a number of state-level statistics, the modes of which clustered around the 50% level. Social Security Administration, *Social Security in America: The Factual Background of the Social Security Act as Summarized from Staff Reports to the Committee on Economic Security* 149–54 (1937).
40. Social Security Administration, Income of the Population 55 or Older, 2010, at 309, 320 (tables 9B6, 10.5), http://www.ssa.gov/policy/docs/statcomps/income_pop55/2010/incpop10.pdf.
41. 514 U.S. 549 (1995).
42. Regan 569.
43. See *Lopez*, 514 U.S. at 564. Justice Kennedy's concurrence, which provided the crucial fifth vote for the majority, suggested that tradition was the crucial factor. Kennedy was reluctant to compromise "the stability of our Commerce Clause jurisprudence as it has evolved to this point," *id.* 574 (Kennedy, J., concurring), and he was particularly troubled by this law because it "seeks to intrude upon an area of traditional state concern." *Id.* 580.
44. National League of Cities v. Usery, 426 U.S. 833 (1976).
45. Garcia v. San Antonio, 469 U.S. 528 (1985).
46. "While we need not adopt a categorical rule against aggregating the effects of any noneconomic activity in order to decide these cases, thus far in our Nation's history our cases have upheld Commerce Clause regulation of intrastate activity only where

that activity is economic in nature." United States v. Morrison, 529 U.S. 598, 613 (2000)..

47. Cooter & Siegel, *Collective Action Federalism* 176–79.

48. *See* Solid Waste Agency of Northern Cook County v. U.S. Army Corps of Eng'rs, 531 U.S. 159 (2001).

49. Balkin 154–55.

50. Erwin Chemerinsky, Constitutional Law: Principles and Policies 277 (4th ed. 2011).

51. See *id.*; National Ass'n of Home Builders v. Babbitt, 130 F.3d 1041 (D.C. Cir. 1997), cert. denied, 524 U.S. 937 (1998); Cargill, Inc. v. United States, 516 U.S. 955, 958 (1995) (Thomas, J., dissenting from denial of certiorari) (arguing that a federal statute regulating private property used by migratory birds "likely stretches Congress' Commerce Clause powers beyond the breaking point"), denying cert. to Leslie Salt Co. v. United States, 55 F.3d 1388 (9th Cir. 1995); United States v. Olin Corp., 927 F.Supp. 1502 (D. Alabama 1996) (invalidating Superfund statute on Commerce Clause grounds), rev'd, 107 F.3d 1506 (11th Cir. 1997).

52. 545 U.S. 1 (2005).

53. See *Lopez*, 514 U.S. at 585 (Thomas, J., concurring).

54. See *id.* 584–602; *Morrison*, 529 U.S. at 627–28 (Thomas, J., concurring).

55. See Thomas W. Merrill, *Bork v. Burke*, 19 Harv. J. L. & Pub. Pol'y 509 (1996).

56. For one example of a development that the framers never imagined, every modern nation-state has assumed some responsibility for environmental protection. See generally David John Frank et al., *The Nation-State and the Natural Environment over the Twentieth Century*, 65 Am. Soc. Rev. 96 (2000).

57. 514 U.S. at 601 n.8 (Thomas, J., concurring).

58. See Utah Highway Patrol Assn. v. American Atheists, 132 S.Ct. 12, 13 (2011) (Thomas, J., dissenting from denial of cert.).

59. Robert A. Dahl, Democracy and Its Critics 112–14 (1989). Rehnquist, the author of *Lopez*, himself once articulated this concern well: "How is this Court to divine what objectives are important? . . . I would have thought that if this Court were to leave

anything to decision by the popularly elected branches of the Government, where no constitutional claim other than that of equal protection is invoked, it would be the decision as to what governmental objectives to be achieved by law are "important," and which are not." Craig v. Boren, 429 U.S. 190, 221 (1976) (Rehnquist, J., dissenting).

60. See David P. Currie, The Constitution of the Federal Republic of Germany 43–46 (1994). "The Basic Law was recently amended to make clear that the question was justiciable, but it remains to be seen whether the horse can be made to drink." David P. Currie, *Subsidiarity*, 1 Green Bag 2d 359, 364 n.35 (1998), citation omitted.

61. Thomas Horsley, *Subsidiarity and the European Court of Justice: Missing Pieces in the Subsidiarity Jigsaw?*, 50 J. Common Market Stud. 267 (2012). The difficulty of judicial enforcement is exacerbated by the fact that the Maastricht treaty's two mentions of the principle seem to point in opposite directions, with one emphasizing devolution and the other aiming at efficiency. See John Peterson, *Subsidiarity: A Definition to Suit Any Vision?*, 47 Parl. Aff. 116, 120 (1994).

62. Anthony Arnull, The European Union and Its Court of Justice 551 (1999). For similar views, see Anthony Arnull et al., Wyatt and Dashwood's European Union Law 162 (4th ed. 2000); Trevor C. Hartley, Constitutional Problems of the European Union 86–88 (1999); Paul D. Marquardt, *Subsidiarity and Sovereignty in the European Union*, 18 Fordham Int'l L. J. 616, 630 (1994).

63. Craig v. Boren, 429 U.S. 190, 221 (1976) (Rehnquist, J., dissenting).

64. Antonin Scalia, *Subsidiarity a l'Americaine: C'est a Dire Preemption*, in Maastricht, Subsidiarity and Italian-EC Relations (The Mentor Group, The Forum for U.S.-EC Legal-Economic Affairs, Venice, 1992), quoted in George A. Bermann, *Taking Subsidiarity Seriously: Federalism in the European Community and the United States*, 94 Colum. L. Rev. 331, 447 n. 464 (1994).

65. Arnull, The European Union and Its Court of Justice 551, quoting United Kingdom v. Council, Case C-84/94 [1996] ECR I-5755, par. 58.

66. See Larry Kramer, *Foreword: We the Judges*, 115 Harv. L. Rev. 4, 143 (2001).

67. I do not claim that this proposal is original. See Cooter & Siegel, *Collective Action Federalism* 181; Balkin 171; Regan 576, 586, 610.

68. Henry J. Kaiser Family Foundation, Kaiser Health Tracking Poll: March 2012, http://www.kff.org/kaiserpolls/8285.cfm. The public is much less enthusiastic about the mandate—only 32% support it—suggesting that they do not understand that you cannot have one without the other.

69. Doonan & Tull 57. The uniqueness of prereform Massachusetts is also emphasized from a different perspective—"everything had already gone wrong" with high health costs and a collapsing market, so the costs of reform were unusually low—in Douglas Holtz-Eakin, *Right Analysis, Wrong Conclusions: Response to Jonathan Gruber*, 30 J. POL. ANAL. & MGMT. 194, 194 (2011).

70. Doonan & Tull 74.

71. Brief of Amicus Health Care for All, Inc., HHS v. State of Florida, 132 S.Ct. 2566 (2012).

72. *See* William F. Danaher, *AFDC and Work: Magnets or Anchors for the Poor?*, 21 SOC. SPECTRUM 33 (2001) (finding no support for the hypothesis); Scott W. Allard & Sheldon Danziger, *Welfare Magnets: Myth or Reality?*, 62 J. POLITICS 350 (2000) (after passage of welfare reform in 1996, 15 states imposed welfare residency requirements in fear of induced migration, despite scant evidence that such migration occurs). The Court long ago noted that such concerns justified a national system of old-age relief: "The existence of…a system [of old-age benefits] is a bait to the needy and dependent elsewhere, encouraging them to migrate and seek a haven of repose. Only a power that is national can serve the interests of all." Helvering v. Davis, 301 U.S. 619, 644 (1937).

73. A study commissioned by Tennessee to explain the rising costs of its program concluded that this was a likely partial explanation. "Given that none of the bordering states offer a program similar to TennCare, it is likely that some individuals may come to Tennessee simply to obtain health insurance coverage.... [A]s long as Tenn-Care offers a program for the uninsurable, and other states do not, there is the continued risk that some individuals will come to Tennessee solely for health care coverage. One might ask if providers

in these bordering states are encouraging patients to relocate to Tennessee in order to access TennCare." William M. Mercer Inc., *Evaluation of Critical Issues Facing the TennCare Program—Report 9* (March 1999). On the cutbacks, see Cyril F. Chang, *Evolution of TennCare Yields Valuable Lessons*, Managed Care, Nov. 2007, at 45.

74. Douglas Wright, *TennCare: A Closer Look* 4–5 (Office of Research, Comptroller of the Treasury, State of Tennessee, Oct. 2001), http://www.tnjustice.org/wp-content/uploads/2011/01/Comptroller-TnCare-Brief-10-01.pdf.

75. *Id.*

76. United States v. Southeastern Underwriters Ass'n, 322 U.S. 533, 552 (1944). The Court here quoted *Federalist* 23: "Not to confer in each case a degree of power commensurate to the end, would be to violate the most obvious rules of prudence and propriety, and improvidently to trust the great interests of the nation to hands which are disabled from managing them with vigor and success." *Id.* 552 n.37.

Chapter 3   Bad News for Mail Robbers

1. David Rivkin, Jr., & Lee A. Casey, *Healthcare Reform vs. the Founders*, Wall St. Journal, Sept. 29, 1993.

2. *Is Government Health Care Constitutional?*, Wall St. J., June 22, 2009.

3. For links to sources not here cited, see Andrew Koppelman, *Origins of a Healthcare Lie*, Salon, May 31, 2012, http://www.salon.com/2012/05/31/origins_of_a_healthcare_lie/.

4. Seven-Sky v. Holder, 661 F.3d 1, 17 (D.C. Cir. 2011), citations omitted.

5. United States v. Lopez, 514 U.S. 549, 567–68 (1995).

6. Paul Clement, *The Patient Protection and Affordable Care Act and the Breadth and Depth of Federal Power*, 35 Harv. J. L. & Publ. Pol'y 887, 889 (2012).

7. The first of these has now been deemed part of American law by a majority of the Court. Roberts was joined by four other justices in the part of his opinion that noted in passing, "The Court today holds that our Constitution protects us from federal regulation

under the Commerce Clause so long as we abstain from the regulated activity."

8. That credit included a front-page profile in the *New York Times.* See Sheryl Gay Stolberg & Charlie Savage, *Vindication for Challenger of Health Care Law,* N.Y. Times, Mar. 26, 2012, A1. When Professor Barnett graciously commented on a draft of this chapter, he emphasized that both the Heritage paper and the Supreme Court brief were collaborative efforts, and that in both documents the independent judgment of his coauthors shaped the structure as well as the details of the arguments.

9. Burroughs v. United States, 290 U.S. 534, 547–48 (1934), quoted in United States v. Comstock, 130 U.S. 1949, 1957 (May 17, 2010).

10. Congressional Record, Dec. 23, 2009, S13830–S13831; Brief of Health Care Policy Scholars as Amici Curiae in support of Petitioners, NFIB v. Sebelius, 32 n.6.

11. Congressional Record, Dec. 22, 2009, S13751–S13754 (Sen. Leahy), S13720–S13721 (Sen. Baucus). The solicitor general cited this debate in his argument, but the dissent, which was confident that the mandate was not a tax, omitted any mention of it.

12. Jacobs & Skocpol 101–20.

13. I focus on Barnett, but many critics of the mandate were Tough Luck Libertarians who had larger ambitions to roll back the New Deal. Richard Epstein, for example, repudiates the idea of guaranteed health care and regards both redistribution and the Civil Rights Act of 1964 as unconstitutional. RICHARD A. EPSTEIN, MORTAL PERIL: OUR INALIENABLE RIGHT TO HEALTH CARE? (1997); RICHARD A. EPSTEIN, FORBIDDEN GROUNDS: THE CASE AGAINST EMPLOYMENT DISCRIMINATION LAWS (1995); Richard A. Epstein, *Impermissible Ratemaking in Health-Insurance Reform: Why the Reid Bill Is Unconstitutional,* Dec. 18, 2009, http://www.pointoflaw.com/columns/archives/2009/12/impermissible-ratemaking-in-he.php. See generally Simon Lazarus, *The Health Care Lawsuits: Unraveling a Century of Constitutional Law and the Fabric of Modern American Government,* American Constitution Society Issue Brief, Feb. 2011, http://www.acslaw.org/node/18259.

14. Randy Barnett, The Structure of Liberty 166 (1998).

15. In the introduction, we noted a similar problem with Nozick.

16. Reid 1–2, 209–12. See also Jane Zhang, *Chronic Condition: Amid Fight for Life, a Victim of Lupus Fights for Insurance*, Wall St. Journal, Dec. 5, 2006.

17. The Structure of Liberty 311.

18. *Id.* 314.

19. *Id.* 200.

20. See Waldron 273, 282–83.

21. The Structure of Liberty 258.

22. *Id.* 276.

23. Jeffrey Winters, Oligarchy (2011).

24. Samuel Freeman, *Illiberal Libertarians: Why Libertarianism Is Not a Liberal View*, 30 Phil. & Pub. Aff. 105 (2001).

25. The Structure of Liberty 182.

26. *Id.* 264n.

27. Nina Totenberg, *Health Care Decision Hinges on a Crucial Clause*, NPR Morning Edition, June 11, 2012, http://www.npr.org/2012/06/11/154583824/health-care-decision-hinges-on-a-crucial-clause.

28. Steven G. Calabresi, *The Originalist and Normative Case Against Judicial Activism: A Reply to Professor Randy Barnett*, 103 Mich. L. Rev. 1081 (2005).

29. Restoring the Lost Constitution, 122.

30. *Id.* 128.

31. *Id.* 126.

32. *Is the Constitution Libertarian?*, 2009 Cato Sup. Ct. Rev. 9, 32.

33. Randy E. Barnett, *Commandeering the People: Why the Individual Health Insurance Mandate Is Unconstitutional*, 5 N.Y.U. J. of L. & Liberty 581, 634 (2010).

34. Brief for Private Respondents on the Individual Mandate, HHS v. State of Florida, 132 S.Ct. 2566 (2012), 8.

35. Florida v. U.S. Dep't of Health and Human Servs., 716 F.Supp.2d 1120 (N.D. Fla. 2010) (refusing to dismiss challenge); 780 F.Supp.2d 1256 (invalidating law); aff'd in part, 648 F.3d 1235 (11th Cir. 2011); Virginia ex rel. Cuccinelli v. Sebelius, 702

F.Supp.2d 598 (E.D. Va. 2010) (refusing to dismiss challenge); 728 F.Supp.2d 768 (invalidating law); rev'd, 656 F.3d 253 (4th Cir. 2011).

36. Thomas More Center v. Obama, 720 F.Supp.2d 882 (E.D. Mich. 2010), aff'd, 651 F.3d 529 (6th Cir. 2011); Liberty Univ. v. Geithner, 753 F.Supp.2d 611 (W.D. Va. 2010), vacated and remanded, 671 F.3d 391 (4th Cir. 2011); Mead v. Holder, 766 F.Supp.2d 16 (D.D.C. 2011), aff'd sub nom. Seven-Sky v. Holder, 661 F.3d 1 (D.C. Cir. 2011).

37. Ezra Klein, *Unpopular Mandate*, The New Yorker, June 25, 2012.

38. 780 F.Supp.2d at 1286.

39. The sentence appears in both *Cuccinelli* opinions: 728 F.Supp.2d at 779, 702 F.Supp.2d at 611.

40. He did grumble, as "an historical aside," that insurance contracts are not part of commerce under what he takes to be the original understanding, but he did not pursue the point. Evidently he was not bold enough to overrule decades-old settled Supreme Court case law.

41. He also relied heavily on the absence of a severability clause in the final version of the law. But as the Eleventh Circuit noted when it reversed him on this, laws are presumed severable, and the Senate and House drafting manuals declare that such clauses are unnecessary.

42. Barnett, *Commandeering the People*, 634. He does not expressly criticize Vinson, but notes that the commandeering argument "might usefully supplement" Vinson's.

43. New York v. United States, 505 U.S. 144, 166 (1992), quoted in Printz v. United States, 521 U.S. 898, 920 (1997).

44. United States v. Sanchez, 340 U.S. 42, 44 (1950). A claim that the tax is a "direct tax"—forbidden by Article I, Section 9—is even more desperate. This was rejected by the Court in a few paragraphs (even the dissenting judges did not argue the contrary), and I will not dwell on it here.

45. This criticism of Judge Vinson's reasoning is made in Gillian Metzger & Trevor Morrison, *Health Care Reform, the Tax Power, and the Presumption of Constitutionality*, BALKINIZATION

(Oct. 19, 2010, 1:50 PM), http://balkin.blogspot.com/2010/10/health-care-reform-tax-power-and.html.

46. Brief for State Respondents on the Minimum Coverage Provision, HHS v. State of Florida, 132 S.Ct. 2566 (2012), 14.

47. The career of the metaphor is traced in James B. Stewart, *How Broccoli Landed on the Supreme Court Menu*, N.Y. Times, June 13, 2012.

48. Judge Hudson's concern was asparagus. *See* Kevin Sack, *Tea Party Shadows Health Care Ruling*, N.Y. TIMES, Feb. 2, 2011, A16. In Mead v. Holder, 766 F.Supp.2d 16, 37 (D.D.C. 2011), the court reports a similar hypothetical by plaintiffs involving wheat.

49. See Cruzan v. Director, Missouri Dept. of Health, 497 U.S. 261 (1990).

50. Frederick Schauer, *Slippery Slopes*, 99 HARV. L. REV. 361 (1985).

51. John Hart Ely, Democracy and Distrust: A Theory of Judicial Review 183 (1980).

52. Brief for State Respondents on the Minimum Coverage Provision, HHS v. State of Florida, 132 S.Ct. 2566 (2012), 12.

53. Ilya Somin argues (in response to earlier writings of mine) that I have underestimated the danger, and that "a purchase mandate can transfer money to a favored industry without requiring additional government spending or tax increases." *A Mandate for Mandates: Is the Individual Health Insurance Case a Slippery Slope?*, 75 L. & Contemp. Probs. 75, 96–98 (2012). But it has not happened, and the reason cannot be the action/inaction distinction, which no one heard of before the ACA.

54. Jared Goldstein, *Broccoli and the Conservative Imagination*, Balkinization, May 1, 2012, http://balkin.blogspot.com/2012/05/broccoli-and-conservative-imagination.html.

55. Ayn Rand, Atlas Shrugged 1070 (Signet 1996).

56. Anne C. Heller, Ayn Rand and the World She Made 50, 57–58, 60 (2009).

57. Florida v. U.S. Dep't of Health and Human Servs., 716 F.Supp.2d 1120, 1162 (N.D. Fla. 2010) (quoting Plaintiff's argument).

58. 197 U.S. 11, 26 (1905).

59. The Supreme Court has noted that, if there were a valid rights-based objection to a federal statute, a state would likewise

be prohibited from enacting that statute. *United States v. Comstock*, 130 S.Ct. 1949, 1956 (2010).

60. Brief for State Respondents on the Minimum Coverage Provision, *HHS v. State of Florida*, 132 S.Ct. 2566 (2012), 33–34.

61. *Id.* 15.

62. *Id.* 38.

63. See Lee Epstein, William Landes, and Richard Posner, *Inferring the Winning Party in the Supreme Court from the Pattern of Questioning at Oral Argument*, 39 J. Leg. Stud. 433 (2010).

64. Steve Peoples, *Health Ruling to Change Campaign*, USA Today, June 28, 2012, http://www.usatoday.com/USCP/PNI/Nation/World/2012-06-28-APUSPresidentialCampaign_ST_U.htm.

Chapter 4   What the Court Did

1. *Rancho Viejo, LLC v. Norton*, 334 F.3d 1158, 1160 (D.C. Cir. 2003) (Roberts, J., dissenting) (denying rehearing en banc).

2. 42 U.S.C.A. 1809(a)(2)(A).

3. Brief for Appellant, *Virginia v. Sebelius*, 656 F.3d 253 (4th Cir. 2011), 32.

4. Brief for Appellants, *Florida v. U.S. Dep't of Health & Human Servs.*, 648 F.3d 1235 (11th Cir. 2011), 38.

5. Brief of United States, *HHS v. Florida*, (No. 11–117), 49.

6. *Id.*, 50.

7. Einer Elhauge, *The Fatal Flaw in John Roberts' Analysis of the Commerce Clause*, The New Republic Online, July 1, 2012, http://www.tnr.com/blog/plank/104554/the-fatal-flaw-in-john-roberts-analysis-the-commerce-clause.

8. This inattention developed when the acting solicitor general, Neal Katyal, was replaced by Verrilli, who took the problem less seriously. See Jeffrey Toobin, The Oath: The Obama White House and the Supreme Court 278 (2012).

9. Gary Lawson & David B. Kopel, *Bad News for Professor Koppelman: The Incidental Unconstitutionality of the Individual Mandate*, 121 YALE L.J. ONLINE 267 (2011), http://yalelawjournal.org/2011/11/08/lawson&kopel.html. They repeated their arguments in an amicus

brief, coauthored with Robert G. Natelson and Guy Seidman, in the Supreme Court.I respond to their argument at Andrew Koppelman, *Bad News for Everybody: Lawson and Kopel on Health Care Reform and Originalism*, 121 Yale L.J. Online 515 (2012), http://yalelawjournal.org/2012/03/06/koppelman.html. They respond in *Bad News for John Marshall*, 121 YALE L.J. ONLINE 529 (2012), http://yalelawjournal.org/the-yale-law-journal-pocket-part/constitutional-law/bad-news-for-john-marshall/. The exchange was provoked by Andrew Koppelman, *Bad News for Mail Robbers: The Obvious Constitutionality of Health Care Reform*, 121 YALE L.J. ONLINE 1 (2011), http://yalelawjournal.org/2011/04/26/koppelman.html.

10. 130 S.Ct. at 1961, citation omitted.

11. Brief of Authors of The Origins 30.

12. The analysis here is developed in greater detail in Andrew Koppelman, *"Necessary," "Proper," and Health Care Reform*, in Nathaniel Persily, Gillian Metzger, & Trevor Morrison, eds., *The Health Care Case: The Supreme Court's Decision and Its Implications* (2013).

13. Their last sentence is correct that the functional equivalent of the mandate would be a tax credit for purchasing insurance. But then they would need to explain, first, why the functional equivalence does not run both ways, thus sustaining the statute that Congress actually passed, and second, why they are sure that the tax credit would have the same behavioral effects.

14. Quoting The Federalist No. 33, at 202 (Clinton Rossiter ed. 1961). In context, Hamilton was caricaturing the views of those who opposed broad federal power under the Necessary and Proper Clause.

15. Randy Barnett, *A Weird Victory for Federalism*, June 28, 2012, http://www.scotusblog.com/2012/06/a-weird-victory-for-federalism/.

16. Ashwander v. Tennessee Valley Authority, 297 U.S. 28, 348 (1936) (Brandeis, J., concurring). See RICHARD H. FALLON, JR. ET AL., HART AND WECHSLER'S THE FEDERAL COURTS AND THE FEDERAL SYSTEM 78–80 (6th ed. 2009). Thanks to Neil Siegel for calling my attention to these sources.

17. Robert D. Cooter & Neil S. Siegel, *Not the Power to Destroy: An Effects Theory of the Tax Power*, 99 Va. L. Rev. 1195 (2012).

18. Cooter and Siegel are among the principal sources of the theory of the commerce power developed in chapter 2, above, and Siegel has specifically defended the constitutionality of the mandate under the commerce power.

19. National Endowment for the Arts v. Finley, 524 U.S. 569, 596 (1998) (Scalia, J., concurring in the judgment), quoting Arkansas Writers' Project, Inc. v. Ragland, 481 U.S. 221, 237 (1987) (Scalia, J., dissenting).

20. 42 U.S.C. § 1396a(a)(10)(A)(i)(VIII).

21. United States v. Winstar Corp., 518 U.S. 839, 872 (1996).

22. Roberts thinks it would be difficult to do that as a practical matter, but it actually would be easy for a statute to declare that Medicaid is terminated as of 11:59 p.m. January 1, and that Medicaid II begins operation, taking up all the functions previously carried out by Medicaid, and rehiring all its administrative staff, at 12:01 a.m. on January 2. It is, of course, possible that some members of Congress would take this as an opportunity to reopen the question of how the funds are allocated, generating huge political difficulties. But they are already free to do that in the normal appropriations process, and it is not clear why the relabeling would exacerbate this perennial problem. Thanks to Senator Tom Daschle for help in thinking through this issue.

23. Betsey Stevenson, *Beyond the Classroom: Using Title IX to Measure the Return to High School Sports*, 92 Rev. of Econ. & Stat. 284 (2010).

24. Nevada v. Skinner, 884 F.2d 445, 448 (9th Cir.1989), quoted in Florida *ex rel.* Bondi v. U.S. Dep't of Health & Human Servs., 780 F.Supp.2d 1256, 1268–69 (N.D. Fla. 2011).

25. Jan Crawford, *Roberts Switched Views to Uphold Health Care Law*, CBS Face the Nation, July 1, 2012, www.cbsnews.com/8301-3460_162-57464549/roberts-switched-views-to-uphold-health-care-law/. Crawford's account is corroborated in Toobin, The Oath 284. Another leak indicated that Roberts also wrote large parts of the dissent, because they had originally been the majority opinion invalidating the law. Paul Campos, *Roberts Wrote*

Both Obamacare Opinions, Salon, July 3, 2012, http://www.salon. com/2012/07/03/roberts_wrote_both_obamacare_opinions/. This claim is less plausible, because the substantive legal theories in the dissent are so different from those in Roberts's opinion.

26. Reuters, *Justice Scalia Steps Up Criticism of Healthcare Ruling,* July 29, 2012, http://www.reuters.com/article/2012/07/29/us-usa-court-scalia-idUSBRE86S0OR20120729.

27. *Siding with the Liberal Wing,* N.Y. Times, June 28, 2012.

28. Jonathan Adler, *Judicial Minimalism, the Mandate, and Mr. Roberts,* in Nathaniel Persily, Gillian Metzger, & Trevor Morrison, eds., The Health Care Case: The Supreme Court's Decision and Its Implications (2013).

29. An oration delivered before the democrats and antimasons, of the County of Plymouth: at Scituate, on the fourth of July, 1836, at 38 (1836).

30. The Structure of Liberty, 143.

31. Jack M. Balkin & Sanford Levinson, *Understanding the Constitutional Revolution,* 87 Va. L. Rev. 1045 (2001).

32. That's why nothing turns on the question, much discussed after the decision, whether his Commerce Clause discussion is holding or dictum.

Chapter 5 Where It Hurts

1. Congressional Budget Office, An Analysis of Health Insurance Premiums Under the Patient Protection and Affordable Care Act, Nov. 30, 2009.

2. Kaiser Comm'n on Medicaid and the Uninsured, The Role of Medicaid in State Economies: A Look at the Research, Jan. 2009, http://www.kff.org/medicaid/upload/7075_02.pdf.

3. N. C. Aizenman & Karen Tumulty, *Medicaid Expansion a Tough Sell to Governors of Both Parties,* Wash. Post, July 12, 2012.

4. Report of the State Budget Crisis Task Force 15–16 (July 2012).

5. Kaiser Commission on Medicaid and the Uninsured, Medicaid Coverage and Spending in Health Reform: National and State-by-State Results for Adults at or Below 133 Percent FPL 10 (May 2010).

6. Letter of Governor Rick Perry to Secretary Kathleen Sebelius, July 9, 2012, http://governor.state.tx.us/files/press-office/O-SebeliusKathleen201207090024.pdf.

7. Manny Fernandez, *Texas Counties Fear Residents Will Pay the Price of Perry's Medicaid Rebuff*, N.Y. Times, July 17, 2012.

8. Corrie MacLaggan, *Is Texas Really Thinking of Opting Out of Medicaid?*, Austin American-Statesman, Nov. 13, 2010.

9. Todd Ackerman & Alexa Walczak, *Feds Rank Texas Worst Healthcare Provider*, Houston Chronicle, July 5, 2012.

10. Benjamin D. Sommers et al., *Mortality and Access to Care Among Adults After State Medicaid Expansions*, 2012 New Eng. J. Med. 1025.

11. The Perryman Group, Only One Rational Choice: Texas Should Participate in Medicaid Expansion Under the Affordable Care Act (Oct. 2012).

12. Douglas Holtz-Eakin, *American Action Forum Analysis Finds Supreme Court's Ruling on Medicaid Will Add Hundreds of Billions to Cost of Affordable Care Act*, June 29, 2012, http://americanactionforum.org/topic/american-action-forum-analysis-finds-supreme-court%E2%80%99s-ruling-medicaid-will-add-hundreds-billion.

13. Congressional Budget Office, *Estimates for the Insurance Coverage Provisions of the Affordable Care Act Updated for the Recent Supreme Court Decision*, July 24, 2012, http://www.cbo.gov/publication/43472.

14. Joey Fishkin, *Whose Gun, Whose Head? Gaming Out the Medicaid Expansion*, Balkinization, July 26, 2012, http://balkin.blogspot.com/2012/07/whose-gun-whose-head.html.

15. Kaiser Comm'n on Medicaid and the Uninsured, A Historical Review of How States Have Responded to the Availability of Federal Funds for Health Coverage, Aug. 2012.

16. Manu Raju, *GOP Lawmakers Urge States on Medicaid*, Politico, June 29, 2012, http://www.politico.com/news/stories/0612/78041.html.

17. In a television interview soon after the Court's decision, Senate minority leader Mitch McConnell repeatedly evaded questions about how he proposed to provide universal coverage. See http://www.tnr.com/blog/plank/104581/uninsured-tough-luck.

Index

universal health care
  under ACA, 32
  emergency room care as
    purported substitute
    for, 13
  Medicaid expansion as, 124
  nearly achieved in Hawaii,
    70
  obstacles to, 69
  opponents of, 162n13
  private charity as purported
    substitute for, 13–14
  success in other countries,
    12, 36
Urbanowicz, Peter, 73–74

V
Verrilli, Donald, 105, 112–113,
    166n8
Vinson, Roger, 91–95, 97, 127–
    128, 131, 164n42
Volokh, Sasha, 12, 75

W
Waldron, Jeremy, 148n10
Wal-Mart, health insurance limits
    at, 29
welfare magnets, 70
White, Nikki, 82–83, 86
Wickard v. Filburn, 56
Wilson, Joe, 75